Crazy Quilt
Décor

J. Marsha Michler

©2005 J. Marsha Michler
Published by

kp books
An imprint of F+W Publications, Inc.

**700 East State Street • Iola, WI 54990-0001
715-445-2214 • 888-457-2873**

Our toll-free number to place an order or obtain a free catalog is 800-258-0929.

The following registered trademark terms and companies appear in this publication: Kreinik™ Silk Serica®

Library of Congress Catalog Number: 2004113674

ISBN: 0-87349-765-1

Edited by Sarah Herman
Designed by Donna Mummery and Marilyn McGrane

Printed in China

Dedication

At the time of the writing of this book my son was serving a year in the U.S. Army in Bagdad, Iraq. Nothing could have caused me more apprehension. This book is dedicated to all who have served this cause.

Acknowledgments

A very many thanks to all at KP Books who have helped make this book a reality including Bill Krause; Julie Stephani; Sarah Herman, editor; Donna Mummery and Marilyn McGrane, layout artists; and Bob Best, photographer. Thanks also to those who have been wonderful in keeping me supplied including Dena Lenham of Kreinik Manufacturing Co. Inc., Vickie Smith of YLI, Vikkie Clayton and Maggie Backman of Things Japanese. And a very special thanks to some very special friends who have helped things along in their own ways including Nina, Bear, Julia, Rod and Raymond. And thanks to John Smith for helping with the doll stands and other woodworks.

Foreword

Crazy ... yes! Join me on this quilting journey, from
Raggy to heirloom we'll travel far. With some
Artful creating and lots of neat stuff to try ... a few
Zany ideas and much more than that, it's
Yetta yetta 'nother thing to stitch! A

Quest is part of this journey, foraging for
Umpteen fabrics and stashing some glamorous stuff.
I'm in here! I say in my sewing space. Get me a
Lantern, must have a good light! And some
Tools, just a few simple things. It's

Decorating! A fun thing to do! Adding lots of
Embellish... what?! "Quilting beauty treatments!" Every
Color of the rainbow and then some, and those
Options and ideas! Gotta have 'em! Let's
Redo the abode, it'll be so grand!

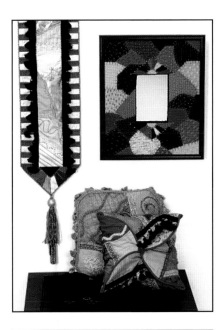

Table of Contents

New and different from my previous books on crazy quilting are some innovative "turns" on methods:

- Work Confetti Piecing so the seams are exposed (Raggy Pillow).
- Use Topstitch Appliqué in one layer (Crazy Lace Curtain and Lite 'N Airy Southwest Throw).
- Learn a stained glass variation of Topstitch Appliqué (Child's Cuddle Quilt).
- Crazy quilt with leather (Crazy Leather Frame).
- Faux crazy quilt (Needlepoint Mirror Frame and Faux Crazy Floor Cloth).
- Collage quilt: A form of crazy quilting in which things are simply layered then stitched (Charmed Napkin Ring and Collage Coasters).
- And a few other things, such as using fabrics for their "ravel" qualities and making your own cording and tassels.

I hope these techniques spark your own ingenuity! And that's the idea: for *you* to turn out something that is uniquely *yours!*

Decorator fabrics offer lots of variety in surface texture and subtle prints. Silk, rayon, wool, cotton and other natural fibers are a pleasure to work with. Add a variety of sew-on trims such as gimps, braids and laces to your collection.

Collecting Fabrics

It's always a good idea to collect fabrics that you like as you find them. Building a stash has its benefits.

Some of the projects call for decorator-type fabrics. Decorator fabrics tend to be heavier than dressmaking types, and are available in a wide range of fibers, colors, textures and finishes. Look for drapery, curtain, slipcover and table linen varieties. Avoid upholstery fabrics backed with a rubbery substance; they are too heavy.

Lovers of crazy quilting can still use the "classics" of the quilting world: printed cotton quilting fabrics for which the Confetti Piecing method was especially designed. You will find many ways to use them throughout this book.

If your project is to be washable, always prewash the materials you will be using. All yardages in the materials listings assume a 44"/45" width unless otherwise indicated.

Fabrics for Foundations

Many of the projects call for a foundation fabric. 100 percent cotton muslin provides a firm base and is appropriate for most projects.

100 percent cotton batiste is lighter than muslin and is soft. Handle with care to keep it from bunching up underneath as you work on it.

Use cotton organdy for a foundation that also acts as a stiffener.

Always wash and press the foundation fabric before using, even if it is said to be prewashed.

Threads for Crazy Quilt Embroidery

With the Antique Method, embroidery is worked along the seams of patches. It holds the patches in place and also provides decoration. Rows of embroidery stitches may be added to other projects as well.

For patch seam embroidery, choose twisted threads which give wonderful texture to the stitches. These come in different thicknesses and are not separated like flosses. Pearl (perle) cottons are the easiest to work with, with size eight being the most common.

For interesting textures, collect chenille, variety threads, fuzzy yarns, metallic braids and silk ribbons. Avoid types that are too thick or delicate to be sewn through fabric.

Workspace

Set up a workspace (if you haven't done so already) with a sewing desk, work table and ironing board. Good lighting is essential. The best light is always daylight, but fluorescent also works well. Fluorescent lights are easier on the eyes than incandescent, and you get more brightness per wattage, representing a savings on the ol' power bill.

Tools, Equipment and Other Necessities

There are "by hand" and "by machine" methods in this book. In any case, most projects are assembled by machine. You will need a sewing machine that is capable of straight stitch and zigzag.

A quality fabric-cutting scissors (shears) is essential. You will also need a tape measure, pins, hand sewing needles in assorted types, a seam ripper, embroidery scissors, a small piece of leather for pulling stubborn hand needles through fabric, a cheaper scissors for cutting paper, pencil and ruler.

A rotary cutter, cutting mat and acrylic straight-edge are needed for the Confetti Piecing method and for making bias-cut strips.

An iron is also essential. I prefer a dry iron and to use a spray bottle for steam. This prevents your fingers from getting scorched. Pressing is best on a padded surface. Either use a padded ironing board cover or terry cloth towel.

For machine and hand sewing, keep a selection of all-cotton, size 50 sewing threads. It is often possible to use neutral colors such as grey and ecru instead of perfect matches. YLI's Select thread is a superb cotton thread excellent for hand sewing and great in the machine as well.

Safety is Precautionary

Always use your tools with care. Pay attention to where your fingers are in relation to needles and blades. Flying and falling scissors are not a good thing either. Slow down, pay attention and take care.

Other Things You May Need

Check the Resources on page 144 for by-mail and Internet sources to obtain supplies that may be difficult to find locally.

Further Information

Read through the Glossary on pages 138-143 for an understanding of many of the terms used in the text. For instance, if an instruction says to "slipstitch," what does this mean? By finding this out, you will be able to enhance your projects with neatly sewn finishes.

For additional embroidery stitches, other patching and piecing methods, oodles of ways to embellish crazy quilt surfaces and more project ideas, see Other Books by this Author, on page 144.

Here are three basic methods for crazy quilting, two by machine and one by hand: Topstitch Appliqué, Confetti Piecing and the Antique Method. Several additional methods are given throughout the book.

Dabble in all of the methods and you will be able to use the one that is most appropriate for your own ideas. Most projects can be adapted to methods other than those given. Feel free to make your own choices!

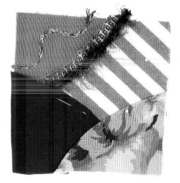

Topstitch Appliqué

Fabrics and trims to make a 6" square.

This method uses a machine sewing. You can make the patches with rounded edges, giving them a softer look.

Collect an assortment of trims such as gimps and braids, cordings, laces, ribbons and anything that can be straight stitched or zigzagged on. Use sewing threads that match or blend.

For the best results, use a firm foundation, such as muslin, and a sheet of paper or other tear-away stabilizer underneath.

1. Roughly cut patches in the sizes and shapes desired. Lay them onto the foundation fabric so that all edges are overlapped by at least 1". Pin.

2. Press under the edges of the overlapped patches ½". Pin.

Optional for a large project: Finish Step 2, then baste each patch about 1" in from the folded edge, leaving the folded edges free so trims can be inserted. If the project is small, this step is unnecessary.

3. Place a sheet of paper or other stabilizer underneath. Find the most underlapped patch and lay a trim along the edge. Sew the trim to the patch. Its ends will be inserted under adjoining patches. Continue, finding the most underlapped patch each time (if you don't, you will be opening up seams later).

4. Once all of the trims have been sewn on, tear away the paper or stabilizer and square up the block (place it on a cutting mat and use a rotary cutter and ruler to even up the edges).

Determine how best to sew each trim. Some can be straight stitched, others, such as cordings, can be zigzagged.

A Basic Pillow with Crazy Quilted Square

Materials

- Crazy quilted square
- Background fabric the size of the pillow (plus 1" for seam allowances)
- Tasseled or other gimp-type trim to go around the crazy quilted square
- 1¼" wide heavy brush fringe to go around the pillow (optional)
- Backing fabric
- Pillow form

(½" seam allowance)

Instructions

1. Center the crazy quilted square on the background fabric and pin.

2. Place trim along the edges of the square and stitch all around. Finish the ends of the trim by butting them together or hemming.

3. Pin the fringe around the edges of the background fabric right sides together.

4. Clip the header of the fringe at each corner to turn the corners neatly and butt the cut ends together.

5. Machine baste the trim to the fabric.

A Simple Pillow Backing

1. Cut a piece of backing fabric the same size as the pillow top.

2. Sew it to the pillow top right sides together, leaving a large opening to insert a pillow form.

3. Turn right-side out and insert the pillow form.

4. Slipstitch the opening closed.

Throw pillows are easy to make, and a square of crazy quilting gives them lots of pizzazz! This pillow features the 6" square made to demonstrate the Topstitch Appliqué method. Make your pillow any size you like. Be sure to add seam allowances. For instance, for a 14" pillow, begin with a 15" square of background fabric.

Overlapped Pillow Backing

Just as simple, although it sounds more complicated, this makes for a neat way to get the pillow form in and out so the pillow cover can be cleaned.

1. Cut the backing fabric 7" longer than the pillow front.

2. Measure up 6" from one end and cut across.

3. Clean finish both cut edges with a zigzag stitch.

4. Fold under the edge of the 6" piece 1" and sew across, stitching next to the zigzagging.

5. Fold under the edge of the larger piece 3" and sew across.

6. Place the larger piece and the pillow top right sides together, then the smaller piece, overlapping the hemmed edges.

7. Sew all around the pillow cover.

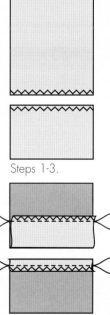

Steps 1-3.

Steps 4-5.

Confetti Piecing

Confetti Piecing is easy to do. Use a rotary cutter, cutting mat and acrylic ruler. Always press the seams to one side after sewing.

Begin with ¼ yard cuts of eight different 100 percent cotton quilting fabrics. Stack them evenly, then cut a 5" piece off one end of the stack.

Note the words ***anywhere you like*** below. Make your cuts anywhere on a block and rejoin anywhere.

(¼" seam allowance)

1. Prepare two blocks,each consisting of four different fabrics. Cut diagonally across one of them.

2. Lay the cut-off piece with right sides together onto the uncut block. Cut along the diagonal edge. Move the cutaway piece aside.

3. Sew together the two pieces that are aligned.

4. Take the other two pieces and align them along their diagonal edges right sides together. Sew them together.

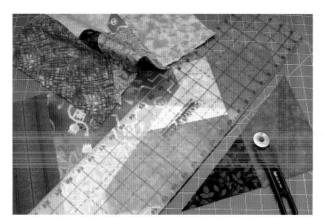

5. Make the next cut ***anywhere you like***.

6. Place the cut piece onto the other block, cut along the edge and sew together the two that are aligned.

7. Note how the two blocks are becoming jumbled. At any point, you may sew the two blocks together and continue to cut and sew until the piece is as jumbled as you like. Repeat the process to make as much Confetti Piecing as needed for your project.

Framing a Crazy Quilt Square

This is a simple way to frame a piece of crazy quilting. This piece is framed without glass. If you prefer to frame under glass, then take your crazy quilt piece to a professional framer, since mats or spacers must be used to keep the textiles away from the glass.

You will need a frame at least 4" larger than the finished square in width and height.

This square demonstrates the Confetti Piecing method. Although this square is left plain, you can quilt, embroider or add embellishments.

Materials

- Crazy quilted square
- Low-loft batting, same size as the square
- Fabric for the backing, same size as the square
- White cotton fabric for the border of the frame
- Glue
- Frame (see Resources on page 144)
- Hanging hardware
- Foam core to fit the frame

Instructions

1. Place the batting on the back of the crazy patched square and place the backing fabric on top of the batting.

2. Place the backing fabric on top and sew around the square, leaving an opening to turn.

3. Turn, press and slipstitch the opening closed.

4. Cut the white cotton fabric about 2" larger all around than the foam core.

5. Center the finished square on the white cotton fabric and tack it in place with a few hand stitches.

6. Place the white cotton fabric with the crazy patched square face down. Place the foam core on top. Make sure the square is centered on the foam core.

7. Fold the edges of the fabric to the back of the foam core and glue them in place.

8. Place the piece in the frame and fasten it in.

9. Add hanging hardware according the manufacturer's instructions.

The Antique Method of Crazy Quilting

The Victorian-era method of patching a crazy quilt is done by hand with embroidery stitches holding the patches in place. My all-time favorite method, it feels "painterly" because the patches can be arranged and rearranged until you like the effect.

You will need fabric shears, sewing or basting thread, needle, pins, fabric scraps, foundation fabric and any desired laces and trims.

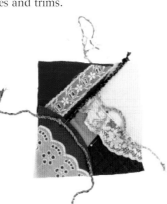

Gather your materials including fabrics, laces, cordings or other trims and a piece of foundation fabric the size of the project plus seam allowances.

1. Roughly cut patches in the sizes and shapes desired. Lay them onto the foundation fabric so that all edges are overlapped by at least ½". Pin.

2. One at a time, pick up a patch and press its overlapped edge under ¼". To press, use a dry iron, spritzing with a spray bottle if necessary. Re-pin. When all of the patches are pressed, add in laces and trims.

3. Hand baste everything in place. If using cordings, stitch them on.

4. Embroider the piece using the twisted embroidery threads of your choice.

Designer's Note

There is no such thing as doing anything just once. Murphy's Law continually teaches me that the first time I try something, it won't work. After a second go, the reason it didn't work on the first try is a mystery. Always, every time. Moral of the story: Have a second go!

A Basic Totebag with Crazy Quilted Pocket

Make one of these and you will see how simple it is! Then you will be able to make a tote in any size, from a small handbag to a large grocery tote. Make the rectangle of fabric the circumference of the bag in width, by somewhat greater than the height of the bag in length. A hem will be formed at the top, and the bottom of the tote will be shaped out of the lower part of the rectangle. Choose a canvas-weight fabric or add a lining to a lighter-weight fabric.

This tote is the right size for going to the library. It started with a rectangle of fabric 27" x 17". It features the 6" square made to demonstrate the Antique Method of crazy patching.

Materials
- Crazy quilted square
- Fabric for the pocket lining, the same size as the crazy quilted square
- A rectangle of fabric for the tote
- A rectangle of fabric the same size for the lining, if needed
- Fabric for the handles
- Cotton fabric for the bias binding

Cutting Instructions
From the cotton fabric for the bias binding:
- Cut 2⅛" wide bias strips for the binding.

(½" seam allowance)

Instructions

1. To make the pocket, place the pocket lining fabric behind the crazy quilted square and pin.

2. Apply bias binding to the upper and lower edges.

3. To make the totebag, place the lining (if desired) behind the rectangle of fabric for the tote and handle the two pieces as one.

4. Bring the sides of the rectangle right sides together and sew a seam.

5. Finish this seam using the method of your choice (I prefer to bias-bind all of the seams, making a neat interior).

6. Center the seam and press the bag, creasing the sides.

7. Sew across the bottom of the bag, then finish this seam.

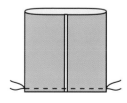

8. One bottom corner at a time, fold the bag, aligning the side crease with the bottom seam, forming a triangular shape.

9. Sew across the triangle evenly (to get this really even, you should measure along both sides of the triangle, mark and sew from one mark to the other).

10. You can leave the triangles as they are, or, for a really nice finish, fold each triangle up against the side of the tote and edge stitch.

11. To finish the top of the bag, apply bias binding to the upper edge. Fold this edge inward 1½" and edge stitch along both edges of the bias binding.

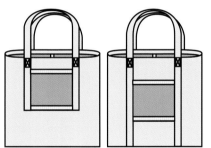

Options for handle placement.

12. Decide the placement of the handles; they can be part-way down the sides of the tote, all the way down to the bottom seam or anywhere in-between. Use a tape measure on the tote to determine your desired length.

13. To make 1" wide handles, cut two pieces of fabric 3" wide by the determined length plus seam allowances.

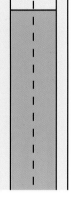

14. Fold in the short ends of each handle ½" and press.

15. Fold in the sides of each handle ½". Press.

16. Fold each handle in half lengthwise.

17. Pin the pocket to the tote.

18. Sew across the bottom binding of the pocket.

19. Pin one of the handles so it laps onto both sides of the pocket. Edgestitch the handle beginning at one end of it and continuing around the top and all the way to the other end.

20. Sew across the end of the handle, then edgestitch the other side of the handle.

21. Repeat Step 19 for the second handle on the other side of the bag (minus the pocket, but you can add a pocket to this side, if you desire).

22. Sew an X pattern on the handles at the top of the bag.

Heart Pattern

Each of the following chapters features a heart such as the one on the right. Make a heart as a small work of art. Use those in this book as inspiration, then adapt the designs to suit your own desires. Hang them on doorknobs, small hooks or on the pullchains of ceiling fans. They make wonderful housewarming gifts!

To make a heart, you will need small scraps of fabrics for crazy patching, muslin for foundation, fabric for backing and any trims and embroidery threads you wish to use, plus a small amount of stuffing.

Instructions

1. Trace and cut out the pattern.

2. Cut one piece from the foundation fabric (or Confetti Piecing) and one from the backing fabric.

3. Work crazy quilting and embellishments on the foundation.

4. Make a hanging cord.

5. Pin the hanging cord on the crazy patched heart so its ends are in the seam allowance.

6. Place the backing on top of the crazy patched heart, right sides together.

7. Sew around the heart, making some extra stitching over the hanging cord to secure it well, and leaving an opening to turn.

8. Turn, press and stuff the heart.

9. Sew the opening closed.

10. Sew on beads, an edging or any additional trims by hand, as desired.

11. Sew a tassel to the bottom.

TOOLBOX

✓ Cordings, page 139
✓ Tassels, pages 142-143
✓ Backing, page 138

← Insert a hanging cord

Heart

¼" seam allowance

Cut 1 of foundation fabric or of Confetti Piecing

Cut 1 of backing fabric

Sew on a tassel

Chapter 1

Far East Odyssey!

Heart of the East

Create a similar heart in the Topstitch Appliqué method. Decorate it with a handmade hanging cord and sewn-on cordings, and edge it with purchased tassel trim. Finish the heart with a Chinese knot tassel.

TOOLBOX

✓ Topstitch Appliqué, page 8   ✓ Heart Pattern, page 15
✓ Cordings, page 139   ✓ Backing, page 138
✓ Chinese Knot Tassel, page 142

Far East Fanfare Quilt ... with Butterflies!

Finished size: 49" in diameter

Materials

- Large piece of paper or newspaper
- Scissors
- Pencil
- Tape measure
- 1¾ yd. muslin for the foundations
- 2 yd. backing fabric
- 5 Chinese knot tassels
- 5 bone rings for hanging

For the Fans

- Tracing paper or a photocopy of the large fan and small fan (see instructions)
- ½ yd. cotton organdy fabric for the large fans
- Pieces of silk and silk blend fabrics in jewel tones
- Metallic braids in gold and silver*
- Cotton cording for welting
- Silk fabric for welting in black

For the Crazy Patched Areas

- Silk fabric scraps in pastel shades
- Rayon threads in light to medium shades*
- Metallic braids and ribbons in assorted colors*
- Hand-dyed spun silk and silk threads*
- Silk ribbons for embroidery

For the Butterflies

- Small pieces of hand-dyed silk fabrics in medium shades
- Rayon thread in black*
- Silk embroidery thread
- Glass seed beads to harmonize with the hand-dyed silk fabrics
- Gold or silver paillettes

*Used in this project: Kreinik metallic braids, YLI Pearl Crown Rayon threads and Victoria Clayton hand-dyed Spun Silk and Silk Perle threads

(½" seam allowance unless otherwise noted.)

Make this quilt for a room that needs a strong focal point. Fans and butterflies are united in this dramatic silk quilt. Strong contrast gives it drama and an op-art effect. Brilliant jewel colors and straight-edged fans are combined with the lighter colors and curved lines of butterflies and crazy patches. All new ideas are experiments. Sometimes they work!

The instructions give a way to assemble this quilt that is more or less foolproof. I call it the "appliqué" method. It removes the guesswork of getting the pieces to fit together properly. This method is in the instructions below, and is a good one to know when you are piecing together complex shapes.

This quilt is designed to be used as a wallhanging, hence the large (outer) fans are pieced onto cotton organdy fabric to give them extra stability. If you'd rather make the quilt as a throw, substitute paper piecing.

TOOLBOX

- ✓ Dyeing Silk, page 20
- ✓ Chinese Knot Tassel, page 142
- ✓ The Antique Method of Crazy Quilting, page 12
- ✓ French Knot, page 140
- ✓ Bullion Stitch, page 140
- ✓ Paper Piecing of Fans, page 141
- ✓ Feather Stitch, page 140
- ✓ Coral Stitch, page 140
- ✓ Welting, page 143
- ✓ Tie the Quilt, page 143

Make the Paper Patterns

1. Make a paper pattern for the large octagon. This is quite large, so tape four sheets of newspaper together.

2. Fold the paper in half lengthwise, then in half again widthwise.

3. Fold the folded edges together to form a triangular shape.

4. Measure along each of the side edges from the point to 19" and mark.

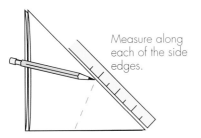

Measure along each of the side edges.

5. Measure between the marks and determine that this edge is an accurate 15". If not, move the line. This is important so the large fans fit correctly.

6. Draw a straight line across (using a ruler) and cut along the line. You can either add ½" seam allowance to the paper pattern or add the allowance when cutting the fabrics. Set the pattern aside.

7. Make a paper pattern for the smaller octagon. Fold the paper using the same method as Steps 2 and 3.

8. Measure along each of the side edges from the point to 9¼" and mark. Check that the line between the marks is an accurate 7¼".

9. Draw a straight line across (using a ruler) and cut along the line. You can either add ½" seam allowance to the paper pattern, or add the allowance when cutting the fabrics.

Patch the Foundation

1. Use the smaller octagon pattern to cut a piece of foundation fabric.

2. Patch the foundation using pastel silk fabrics and the Antique Method of patching.

Layout diagram of the quilt.

Make the Butterflies

1. Trace and cut out the butterfly pattern.

2. Cut three butterflies from the hand-dyed silks.

3. Press the outer edges under, clipping as indicated on the pattern.

4. Scrunch the center together, place it on the quilt and sew over the scrunched center several times.

5. Arrange the wings as you like and pin. Slipstitch all around.

6. Embroider along the patch edges using rayon and metallic threads.

7. When the embroidery along the patched edges is finished, add embroidery to the butterflies.

8. Using black thread, stitch over the center of the butterfly several times.

9. Add some French knots for the head.

10. Use the outline stitch to make antennae, adding French knots to the ends.

11. Make the abdomen of the butterfly out of a long bullion stitch.

Decorate the butterflies as you like. These have a metallic thread outline with random seed beads. The lines are in dark shades of silk thread. A row of beaded sequins finishes each wing.

Make and Add the Small Fans

1. Make eight tracings or photocopies of the small fan.

2. Sew the fans following the Paper Piecing of Fans instructions.

3. Trace and cut out the small fan center.

4. Cut eight small fan centers out of fabric.

5. Press under the upper edges and slipstitch one center to each fan.

6. Press the upper edges of the fan under ½".

7. Press under the outer edge of the smaller octagon ½".

8. Place a fan under each edge. Pin, then slipstitch. (This is an alternative method to machine sewing for greater accuracy).

Add the Small Octagon to the Large

1. Cut a piece of foundation and one of backing fabric the same size as the large octagon pattern. Set aside the backing.

2. Pin the smaller octagon/fan piece onto the foundation, centering it carefully. Be sure the sides of the two octagons line up.

3. Baste, leaving the fans loose so that the patches can be placed under their edges. Optional: Later, after the fans are sewn in place, trim away the area of foundation that is under the smaller octagon, leaving approximately ½" seam allowance. Patch the visible area of the larger octagon. Make and add several butterflies if desired. Embroider as before.

Make and Add the Large Fans

1. Trace or photocopy the large fan pattern.

2. Trace or photocopy to make the second half of the fan.

3. Tape the two pieces together.

4. Cut eight large fans out of cotton organdy and eight large fans out of backing fabric, adding ½" all around for seam allowances. Set aside the backing pieces.

5. Carefully and accurately trace the blade stitching lines onto the organdy pieces.

6. Follow the paper piecing instructions to piece the fans onto the organdy (instead of paper).

7. Trace and cut out the large fan center pattern.

8. Use the pattern to cut eight centers.

9. Fold the upper edges of the fan to the back ½" and press.

10. Fold and press pleats into the fans as indicated on the pattern.

11. Pin, then slipstitch each fan center to the pieced blades leaving the "wings" of the pleats free.

12. Embroider along the fan blades using metallic braid and the feather stitch. Work the coral stitch along the tops of the fan centers (again, leaving the "wings" of the pleats free).

13. Make welting and machine baste it to the outer edge of each large fan.

14. Sew a backing onto each fan right sides together. Turn right-side out and press.

15. Sew the large fans to the large octagon the same way as for the small fans. Press the seams toward the quilt.

The centers of the large fans are pleated.

Trace the fan pattern directly onto cotton organdy fabric.

Silk Fabrics and Hand Dyeing Silk

Silk is the fiber of choice for a quilt such as this one. Silk is way at the top of a "fiber luxury" list. Affordable, lightweight and drapable, easy to dye, capable of nonstop manipulation (excellent for pleats, tucks, wrinkling, etc.); really and truly, nothing surpasses this fiber.

Dyeing silks is covered in "The Magic of Crazy Quilting." Purchase a yard of silk fabric, some silk dyes and never be lacking in colors, not to mention special effects, such as mottling. Dyeing silk is very simple and quick (see Resources on page 144).

Finish the Quilt

1. Press under the edges of the quilt backing. Place it on the back of the quilt and pin. Slipstitch all around the large octagon.

2. Tie the quilt.

3. Make and sew on five Chinese knot tassels.

4. Sew a bone ring to the back of each of the five uppermost fans for hanging.

5. Place small nails in the wall to match the bone ring placements.

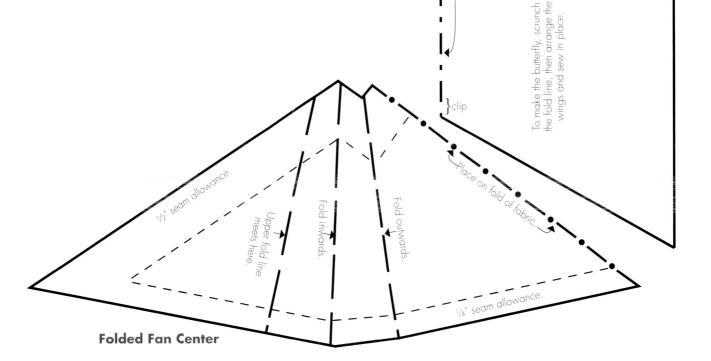

}clip

Place on fold of fabric.

Butterfly

½" seam allowance included

To make the butterfly, scrunch the fold line, then arrange the wings and sew in place.

}clip

Place on fold of fabric.

½" seam allowance.

Upper fold line meets here.

Fold inwards.

Fold outwards.

¼" seam allowance.

Folded Fan Center

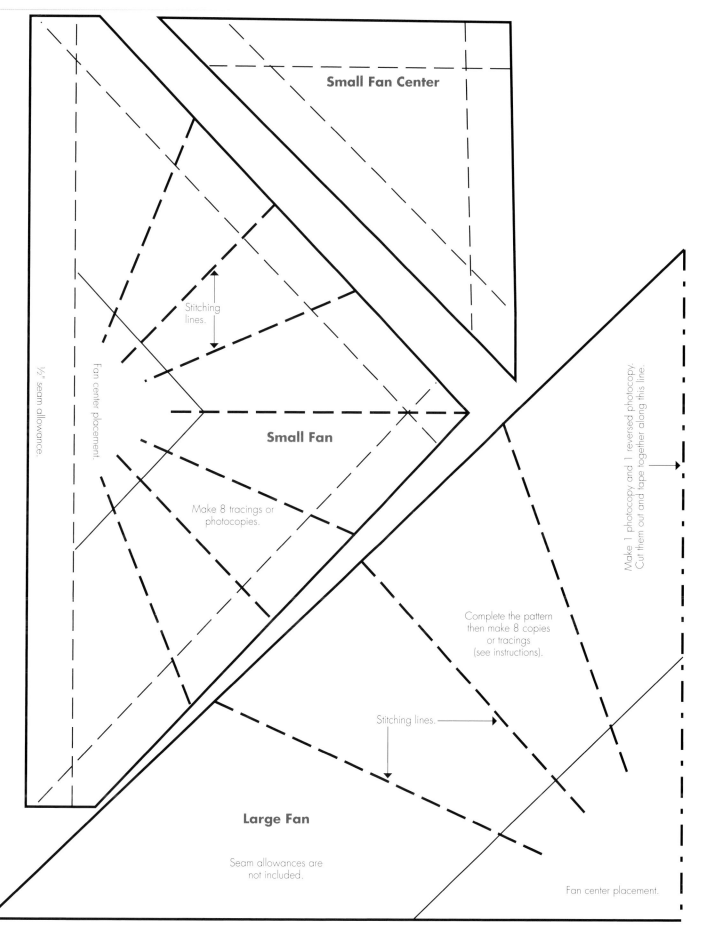

Small Fan Center

Stitching
lines.

½" seam allowance.

Fan center placement.

Small Fan

Make 8 tracings or
photocopies.

Make 1 photocopy and 1 reversed photocopy.
Cut them out and tape together along this line.

Complete the pattern
then make 8 copies
or tracings
(see instructions).

Stitching lines.

Large Fan

Seam allowances are
not included.

Fan center placement.

Exotic Fans Bellpull

Finished size: 7¼" x 47¾"

Materials

- ⅓ yd. muslin for the foundation
- Small pieces of hand-dyed and commercial silk fabrics in pastels and off-whites
- Narrow trims such as cotton laces, Venice, self-made cordings and narrow ribbons
- Sew-on or iron-on metallic ribbons and braids*
- ⅛ yd. each of two contrasting silk fabrics (I used fuschia and off-white dupionni)
- 2¼ yd. tasseled trim in black (or color of your choice)
- ¼ yd. backing fabric
- 3½ yd. self-made or purchased cording, gold
- Wooden bead, painted metallic gold
- 2 Chinese coin replicas
- Bone ring or loop for hanging
- Quilting thread (optional)
- Pearl cotton or other thread for tying
- White glue

For the Two Small Fans
- Small piece of organdy fabric
- Scraps of silk fabrics in jewel tones
- Iron-on metallic ribbon, gold*

*Used in this project: Kreinik metallic ribbons and braids

(½" seam allowances)

Cutting Instructions

From the muslin for the foundation:
- One piece 5¼" x 41" for the center
- Two pieces 4" x 41" each for the side panels

From the backing fabric:
- One piece 8¼" x 49"

TOOLBOX
- ✓ Fabrications, pages 139, 141
- ✓ Topstitch Appliqué, page 8
- ✓ Paper Piecing of Fans, page 141
- ✓ Rod Pocket, page 142
- ✓ Cordings, page 139
- ✓ Dyeing Silk, page 20
- ✓ Tie the Quilt, page 143

Like the Far-East Fanfare Quilt, this bellpull relies on the element of contrast for its dramatic appeal. Bellpulls make wonderful room accent pieces, especially where there is limited wall space. This one is crazy patched in the Topstitch Appliqué method.

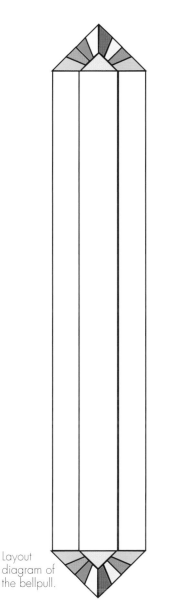

Layout diagram of the bellpull.

Patch the Fabric

1. With the pastel and off-white silk fabrics, make some fabricated patches.

2. Patch the wider of the three muslins using these patches and the pastel silk fabrics in the Topstitch Appliqué method.

3. Apply trims to the patch edges and across some of the patches.

4. Cut the two contrasting silk fabrics into 4" wide strips and sew them to make two pieces the size of the muslin side panels foundations.

5. Baste the strips to the muslin side panels.

6. Sew the two striped sections and the crazy patched section right sides together. Press the seams towards the outer edges.

7. Sew the tasseled trim over the seams just sewn.

Make and Add the Small Fans

1. To make two small fans, trace the small fan pattern on page 21 onto the organdy fabric.

2. Follow the paper piecing method, but piece the jewel-toned silk fabrics onto the organdy instead of paper.

3. Cut out and add a fan center to each fan.

4. Apply iron-on metallic trims along the seam lines using a double row along the fan center.

5. Sew one fan to each end of the bellpull.

Finish the Bellpull

1. Place the backing fabric and bellpull right sides together and pin.

2. Trim the backing to match the fans at the top and bottom. Sew around the bellpull, leaving an opening to turn.

3. Turn, press and slipstitch the opening closed.

4. If desired, machine quilt in a freeform pattern along the striped sections.

5. Tie the piece.

6. Hand sew the gold cording, beginning and ending at the bottom of the lower fan, leaving the long ends.

7. Tie the cordings together into an overhand knot.

8. Slide the wooden bead up to the knot and squeeze glue inside the bead. Allow to dry.

9. Trim the tassel ends to about 4½".

10. Tie two Chinese replica coins to two of the tassel strands.

11. To hang the bellpull, sew a rod pocket and insert a dowel, or sew a bone ring to each side of the upper fan back.

Knot two Chinese coin replicas ino the strands.

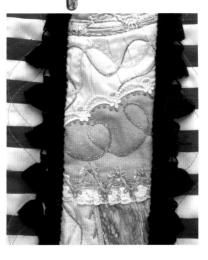

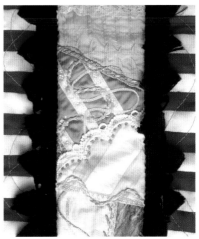

The pastel shades of the silk fabrics and the trims result in an effect that seems nearly painterly. Iron-on metallic trims enhance the embroidery.

Needlepoint Mirror Frame

Finished size: 12" x 14"

Materials

- Wool yarn* (see the sidebar for colors and quantities)
- 15" x 17" piece of 14-count needlepoint canvas
- Pencil
- Ruler
- Tapestry needle
- Rayon thread, gold*
- 4mm beads in pale gold
- Beading thread
- Beading needle
- 12" x 14" piece of foam core
- Craft knife
- Ruler
- Strong thread
- Black acrylic paint
- Small brush
- Glue
- Mirror
- 12" x 14" frame

*Used in this project: Paternayan Persian wool yarn and YLI Pearl Crown Rayon thread

Colors

Choose nine or more main colors plus one, two or three darker or lighter shades of each color. The main colors used here include: golden yellow and sunny yellow for the fan center; black, steel grey, dark violet, hot pink, Chinese red, dark rose, turquoise, off-white and faded dark green for the accents.

Quantities

One or two skeins per color, depending on usage, should be sufficient.

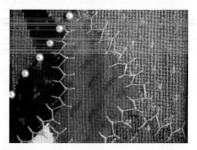

Mix colors for a mottled effect or work simple patterns.

Faux crazy quilting has a charm of its own. You decide on the shapes and sizes of the patches, making this similar to the Antique Method of crazy patching. To create an interesting and vibrant surface for each patch, collect a color plus one to three more shades of it. Then work the needlepoint using all of the shades in each patch as you work. Decide how to stitch each "patch" as you begin to work on it. Try stripes, dots, small squares or random mottling.

TOOLBOX
✓ Feather Stitch, page 140

Prepare the Canvas

1. Draw a 12" x 14" outline, centering it on the canvas.

2. Measure in 4" from each edge and draw a 4" x 6" outline for the mirror placement.

3. Sketch the outlines of the fans using a ruler to draw the lines.

4. Sketch the patch outlines.

Begin the Needlepoint

1. Work needlepoint in the stitch or stitches of your choice. I simply used half cross stitch, but you may like to experiment by using several different needlepoint stitches for the "patches."

2. Stitch around the mirror opening with any dark color of wool.

3. Complete the needlepoint.

Embellish the Frame

1. With gold rayon thread, work the single feather stitch along the edges of the "patches."

2. Sew beads along the outer edges of the fans and fan centers.

Assemble the Mirror and Frame

1. Block the needlepoint as follows.

2. Tack or nail the needlepoint to a board, then steam it. To steam, hold the steam iron above the piece or dampen a press cloth and lay it on the piece, then very lightly run the iron over it. Allow the piece to dry completely before removing the nails or tacks.

3. In the area of the mirror opening, cut the canvas in an "X" shape. Using the craft knife, cut a 4" x 6" corresponding opening in the foam core.

4. Place the foam core on the back of the needlepoint. Fold the edges of the canvas to the back.

5. Thread a needle with a long length of heavy thread and secure by stitching back and forth from side to side, then from top to bottom.

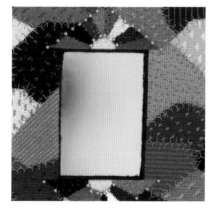

6. Carefully dab black paint around the mirror opening to conceal the canvas and the foamcore.

7. Frame the piece or have it done professionally, placing a mirror behind the opening.

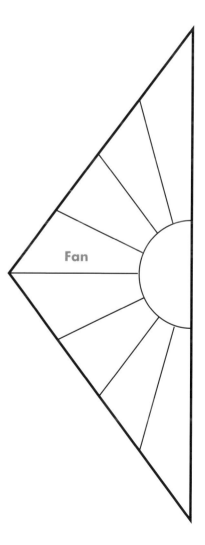

Fan

Ottoman Cover

Why have a plain ottoman sitting around when you can have a fancy, covered ottoman? Such a cover can be either fitted or "au natural." You can make it as a flat piece and just throw it over the ottoman, or shape the edges to make it more tailored.

Materials

- Newspaper
- Pencil
- Scissors
- Muslin for the foundation, same size as the paper pattern
- Lining fabric, same size as the paper pattern
- ¼ yd. fabric for the fans (choose a crisp fabric that creases well)
- ¼ yd. fabric for the fan lining
- 2 handmade Chinese knot tassels
- Scraps for the patches
- Cordings (purchased or hand made)
- Assorted decorator trimmings
- Tassel edging to go around the cover

(½" seam allowance)

Fabrics and cordings readied for the Topstitch Appliqué method of crazy patching.

TOOLBOX

✓ Topstitch Appliqué, page 8
✓ Cordings, page 139
✓ Chinese Knot Tassel, page 142
✓ Fabrications, pages 139, 141
✓ Backing, page 138

Make the Pattern

1. Measure the ottoman to find the desired length and width of the cover, having the same amount of overhang on each side.

2. Make a newspaper pattern this size, adding a ½" seam allowance to the outer edge.

3. Round the corners of the pattern.

4. Drape the pattern over the ottoman to be sure it fits correctly.

5. Use the pattern to cut one piece from the muslin and one piece from the backing fabric.

Make and Add the Fans

1. Cut two pieces each 7" x 22" from the fabric for the fans.

2. Cut two pieces the same dimensions from the fabric for the fan lining.

3. Place a lining and a fan fabric piece right sides together and sew around them, leaving an opening to turn.

4. Turn, press and slipstitch the opening closed.

5. Repeat Steps 3 and 4 for the second fan.

6. Form pleats along the length of each rectangle by folding the piece back and forth until it is all pleated.

7. Press the folds of the pleats.

8. Edgestitch along each fold.

9. Draw together the bottom edge of each fan and stitch all pleats together about 1" up from the bottom of the fan.

10. Lay a fan on each side of the foundation fabric piece and make a pencil line around each fan to indicate placement. Remove the fans.

Embellish the Ottoman Cover

1. Patch the muslin in the Topstitch Appliqué method using the cordings and some fabricated patches.

2. In each of the fan areas, place a fabric in a color that contrasts with the fans, making it slightly larger than the fans.

Assemble the Cover

1. With right sides together, sew the backing to the cover. If desired, fold the corners of the cover into pleats and stitch them in place.

2. Edge the cover by sewing on tassel fringe.

3. Tack the fans in place with hand stitches.

4. Stitch a Chinese knot tassel onto each fan.

See Fabrications in the Glossary for ways to make designed fabrics that will add interest and texture to your projects. Note the pintucked and checkerboarded fabrics used in the photos at left.

Pleat and stitch the corners before applying the edging to make a neatly fitting cover.

Four-Petal Pillow

A clever design, this is a pillow cover made in a flat piece that is then folded over an inner pillow. The method of folding creates a petal-like design. The pillow shown measures 10" across. Follow the instructions to make a pillow the size of your choice.

Materials

- Paper or newspaper
- Pencil
- Scissors
- Muslin for the foundation
- Fabric for the lining
- Scraps for the patches
- Trims
- Embroidery threads of your choice
- Fabric for the insert
- Poly stuffing
- 4 snap fasteners or hook and loop tape

TOOLBOX

✓ Topstitch Appliqué, page 8   ✓ Welting, page 143   ✓ Fabrications, pages 139, 141

Make the Paper Pattern

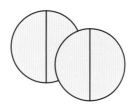

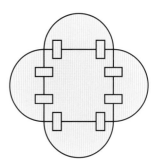

1. Determine the desired finished size of the pillow and make a square this size out of paper or newspaper.

2. Make two circles the same size (diameter) as the square.

3. Cut the circles in half.

4. Tape one half circle to each side of the square.

5. This is the pattern: add seam allowances as you cut out the fabric. Cut one piece out of the muslin and one piece out of the lining fabric.

Patch the Pillow

1. Patch the muslin foundation piece in the Topstitch Appliqué method, adding trims and some fabricated patches. If desired, work some embroidery stitches.

2. Measure completely around the piece and make a welting this length.

3. Pin and baste the welting to the patched top. Sew the lining to the patched muslin right sides together, leaving an opening to turn.

4. Turn, press and slipstitch the opening closed.

Make the Pillow Insert

1. Cut two pieces the same size as the square paper pattern plus seam allowances.

2. Sew the two pieces right sides together, leaving an opening to turn.

3. Turn and stuff the pillow with poly stuffing.

4. Stitch the opening closed.

Cover the Pillow

1. Fold the pillow cover over the insert one flap at a time, so they overlap consecutively.

2. Mark placements for snap fasteners or hook and loop tape and sew them on.

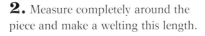

Pillow back.

Position snap fasteners to hold the petals in place.

Octagon Pillow

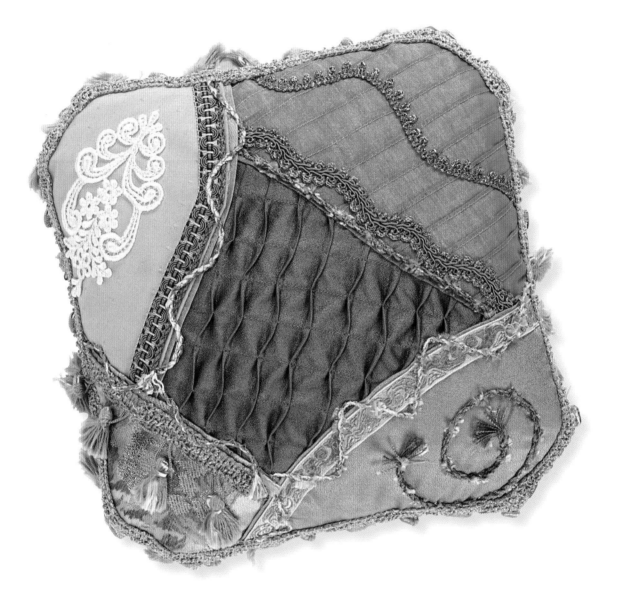

Fancy throw pillows are easy to make. This octagon is simply a square of fabric with its corners removed. This one is 12" across, but make this pillow any size you like! Note how pintucked fabrics add texture to the pillow.

Materials for the Octagon Pillow

- Muslin for the foundation in a square the size desired
- Scraps for the patches
- Trims as desired
- Cotton fabric for the inner pillow
- Poly stuffing
- Fabric for the backing
- Tasselled trim to go around the pillow (optional)

TOOLBOX

✓ Topstitch Appliqué, page 8   ✓ Fabrications, pages 139, 141   ✓ Backing, page 138

Make the Pillow Cover

1. Cut a piece of muslin into a square the size desired, plus seam allowances.

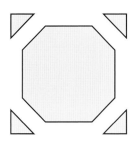

2. Evenly lop off the corners of the muslin to make an octagon.

3. Using the muslin as a pattern, cut two pieces from the cotton fabric for the insert and one piece from the backing fabric.

4. Patch and trim the muslin using the Topstitch Appliqué method and some fabricated patches.

Option: Sew a tasseled trim to the outer edge, staying away from the seam and seam allowance area.

Make the Pillow Insert

1. Sew the two pieces of cotton fabric for the insert together, leaving an opening to turn.

2. Turn and stuff with the poly stuffing.

3. Slipstitch the opening closed.

Finish the Pillow

1. Sew the backing fabric to the pillow top, being careful to keep the tasseled trim free of the stitching. Leave an opening for the insert.

2. Turn it right-side out, add the insert and hand stitch the opening closed.

Drapery Banding

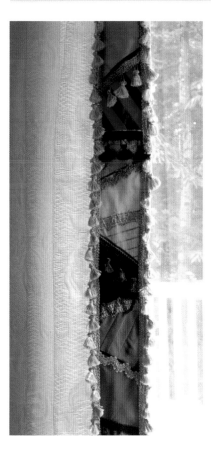

Rather than crazy quilt a whole curtain, consider adding a banding to the outer, inner, upper or lower edges. It's quick and adds an elegant touch!

1. Make a banding the length and width desired (the one shown here is 4" wide).

2. Cut the foundation to the exact width desired and add ½" seam allowances to each at the top and bottom.

3. Patch the foundation in the Topstitch Appliqué method, adding trims and embroidery as desired and using some fabricated patches.

4. Zigzag the side edges.

5. Fold in and press the seam allowances at the top and bottom.

6. Machine baste the piece along its side edges to the curtain.

7. Sew on ½" wide trim to cover the zigzagging, sewing along both edges to fasten the banding to the curtain.

8. Slipstitch the top and bottom edges to the curtain.

TOOLBOX

✓ Bandings, page 138
✓ Topstitch Appliqué, page 8

✓ Fabrications, pages 139, 141

Japanese Bottomless Money Purse

What's a purse doing in a book about décor? Well, you can use the purse, but its real intention is as a symbol. Imagine a money bag in which there is a constant and steady supply of coins!

Use such a symbol as part of your décor. Mine is in my abundance corner (Feng Shui). Make it in blues and purples (abundance colors) and tie it with gold cord. Stuff it with tissue to make it appear fat and bountiful and add some coins.

Materials

- Tracing paper
- Pencil
- Fabric for the foundation
- Silk fabric scraps for the patches
- Trims
- Silk fabric for the lining
- 2 yd. cording

(¼" seam allowance)

TOOLBOX

✓ Topstitch Appliqué, page 8 ✓ Fabrications, pages 139, 141 ✓ Cordings, page 139

Patch the Fabric

1. Trace and cut out the pattern.

2. Using the pattern, cut four from the foundation fabric and four from the silk fabric for the lining.

3. Patch the foundation pieces in the Topstitch Appliqué method using the silk fabric scraps, trims and some fabricated patches.

Assemble the Patches and the Lining

1. Prepare each of the four patched pieces and the four lining pieces by zigzagging between the dots, as shown on the pattern.

2. Sew the four patched pieces right sides together, sewing from the bottom up to the lower dot. Turn right-side out.

3. Place one lining piece and one bag flap right sides together. Sew between the upper dots. Repeat to sew all four lining pieces to the bag.

4. Sew the lining bottoms right sides together up to the lower dot, leaving an opening in one of the seams to turn. Turn the entire thing right-side out. Press.

5. Slipstitch the opening closed and push the lining down inside the bag.

6. Sew the casing lines as shown on the pattern.

7. Cut two pieces of cording each 30" long.

8. Attach a safety pin to the end of one cord, and run the cord through all of the casings. Knot the ends of the cord together.

9. Attach the pin to the remaining cord and thread it through all of the casings beginning at the opposite side of the bag. Knot.

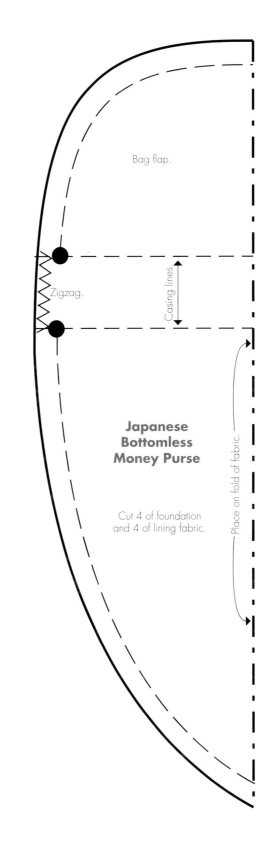

Bag flap.

Zigzag.

Casing lines

Japanese Bottomless Money Purse

Cut 4 of foundation and 4 of lining fabric.

Place on fold of fabric.

Chapter 2

Western Wanderings!

Heart of the West

Make this heart of quilted Confetti Piecing. Decorate it with meandering self-made cording, silver buttons and a bit of leather fringe (make this by snipping a rectangle of leather). Finish it by stitching on a looped-bead fringe and a tassel made out of heavy cotton yarn plus some wildly misbehavin' variety yarn.

TOOLBOX

✓ Confetti Piecing, page 10	✓ Heart Pattern, page 15
✓ Cordings, page 139	✓ Tassels, page 142
✓ Backing, page 138	✓ Looped Fringe, page 138

Western Piano Shawl

Finished size: 37¾" square, not including the fringe.

Materials

- 1 yd. 100 percent cotton batiste fabric for the foundation
- Rayon challis and silk fabrics for the patches, including textured solids and a few subtle prints
- ¼ yd. plain silk fabric for the hand-dyed silk florals
- Silk dyes
- Rayon embroidery threads in a variety of colors*
- Hand-dyed spun silk embroidery threads*
- Materials of your choice for hand-made cordings such as silk ribbons, metallic ribbons and braids, rayon and other threads
- 1 yd. rayon fabric for the borders
- ¼ yd. rayon fabric for the border appliqués (complimentary to the rayon for the border)
- Small piece of lightweight cardboard
- 1 yd. silk or cotton fabric for the backing (54" wide)
- 4½ yd. rayon chainette fringe (4")

*Used in this project: YLI Pearl Crown rayon embroidery threads, Victoria Clayton hand-dyed Spun Silk embroidery threads

(¼" seam allowance)

The style of this shawl/wallhanging is borrowed from the Piano Shawl shown in my first book on crazy quilting, "The Magic of Crazy Quilting." The choice of materials make this a wonderful drapey hanging, wearable shawl or throw. Rayon challis fabric has fairly substantial weight to it, along with a drape that is fluid and elegant. In this western-style shawl, I've combined silks with rayon fabrics; the two fabric types are very compatible.

To retain the drape of the rayon fabrics, use 100 percent cotton batiste for the foundation.

Embellish the shawl with ribbonworked florals made of hand-dyed silk fabric, self-made cording and silk ribbon embroidery. Embroider the shawl using your favorite stitches. My all-time favorite is French knots; I just can't make enough of 'em! Use a quilter's embroidery hoop for working the embroidery.

Choose "western" colors such as leathery browns, sand, sage, black, deep red and gunmetal grey, with a dark brown or black fringe.

TOOLBOX

- ✓ The Antique Method of Crazy Quilting, page 12
- ✓ Rod Pocket, page 142
- ✓ Appliqué, page 138
- ✓ Cordings, page 139
- ✓ Dyeing Silks, page 20
- ✓ Outline Stitch, page 140

Layout diagram of the piano shawl.

Patch the piano shawl.

Use hand-dyed ribbons to sew the flowers.

Add ribbon flowers and cordings to the shawl.

Patch the Foundation

1. Cut one 29¾" square from the batiste for the foundation.

2. Patch the foundation in the Antique Method. I used a "landscaping" effect, suggesting rolling hills.

Dye and Sew Silk Flowers

1. Cut 2"-3" x 9" bias strips out of the plain silk fabric.

2. Dye them in shades that harmonize with the patches.

3. To make the flowers, sew the short ends of the bias strips together, then gather one edge tightly.

4. Place them on the shawl as desired and hand sew them while turning under the outer edge of each.

Embellish the Piano Shawl

1. Make some cordings and arrange them on the shawl.

2. Invisibly hand stitch them in place.

3. Add French knots to the centers of the flowers and some silk ribbon embroidered leaves.

4. Embroider along the edges of the patches using the rayon and silk embroidery threads and silk ribbons. Refer to the photos for embroidery ideas.

Add the Borders

1. Cut two side borders, each 4¾" x 29¾".

2. Sew them to the sides of the shawl.

3. Cut two borders, each 4¾" x 38¼" for the top and bottom.

4. Sew them to the top and the bottom of the shawl.

Appliqué

1. Cut one 2⅜" square from the cardboard.

2. Using the cardboard as a pattern, cut 32 squares from the rayon fabric for the appliqué, making them about 1" larger than the cardboard square.

3. Using a dry iron, place the cardboard square on the back of one of the rayon squares and press the edges of the fabric onto the cardboard (this insures that the appliqué squares will all be accurate and the same). Repeat for all of the rayon squares.

4. Pin the rayon squares onto the borders so they are centered and ½" apart.

5. Slipstitch each of the appliqués in place.

Finish the Piano Shawl

1. Pin the fringe right sides together on the outer edge of the border, all around.

2. Trim off the excess fringe and butt the cut ends together.

3. Machine baste the fringe.

4. Cut a 38¼" square from the backing fabric.

5. Lay the backing fabric on the shawl right sides together. Stitch around, leaving an opening for turning. Take care that none of the fringe gets caught up in the stitching.

6. Turn, press and slipstitch the opening closed.

7. Choose your method of tying. I used black rayon thread and added short meandering lines of the outline stitch to the surface of the shawl, which made a neat backstitch on the reverse. Pull thread ends between the layers so there are no ends hanging.

8. Add a rod pocket if you are using the shawl as a wallhanging. I placed my rod pocket diagonally so the shawl can hang as a draped piece.

Wild West Bellpull

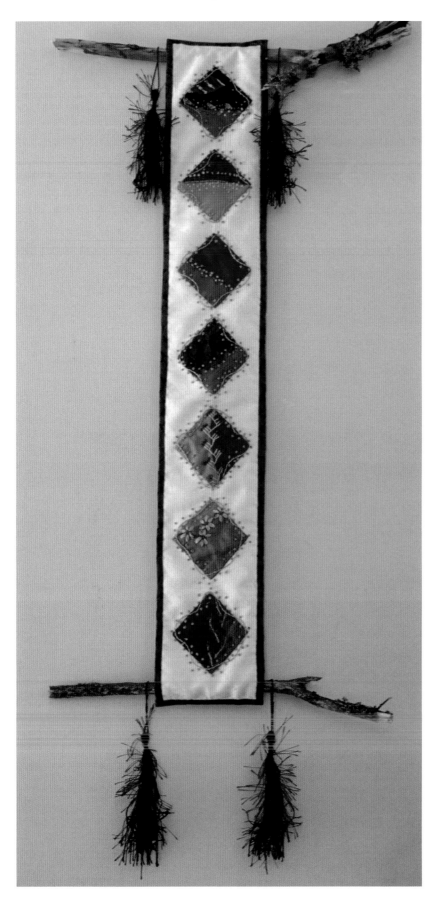

The design of this bellpull matches the Western Piano Shawl's border. Use leftover fabrics from the shawl or collect rayon fabrics to achieve a similar effect. The crazy patching is very simple, consisting of only two patches for each square. The combination of hanging it on weathered sticks and the "hairy" tassels give it a wild look!

Finished size: 5" x 30"

Materials

- ¼ yd. muslin for the foundation
- Small piece of lightweight cardboard
- Scraps of rayon fabric
- ¼ yd. cream-colored cotton or rayon fabric for the background
- Rayon threads in several colors*
- Silk ribbons for embroidery
- Threads for tassels including a "hairy" novelty yarn
- ¼ yd. cotton fabric for the backing
- Cotton or rayon fabric for the bias binding
- 2 weathered sticks

*Used in this project: YLI Pearl Crown Rayon threads

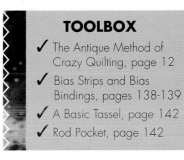

TOOLBOX

✓ The Antique Method of Crazy Quilting, page 12
✓ Bias Strips and Bias Bindings, pages 138-139
✓ A Basic Tassel, page 142
✓ Rod Pocket, page 142

Patch the Appliqué Squares

1. Cut one 5" x 30" piece from each of the following: background fabric, muslin for the foundation and backing fabric.

2. Cut one 2⅝" square from the cardboard.

3. Using the cardboard pattern, cut seven squares from the muslin, making them about 1" larger than the cardboard square.

4. Using the Antique Method of patching, patch each muslin square using the fabric scraps.

5. Place the cardboard on the back of one of the patched squares and press the seam allowance to the back. Repeat for the remaining squares.

Assemble the Bellpull

1. Arrange the squares evenly on the background fabric, placing them ½" apart. Pin, then slipstitch.

2. Embroider along the edges of the patches and around the squares, using the rayon threads and silk ribbons.

3. Place the muslin piece on the back of the bellpull, then add the backing fabric. Pin.

4. Cut the fabric for the bias binding 1⅛" wide and follow the bias binding instructions to bind all of the edges.

5. Make four tassels about 6" long (not including the hanging cord) following the basic tassel instructions.

6. Make a rod pocket for both the top and bottom of the bellpull out of muslin.

7. Place the two weathered sticks through the rod pockets.

8. Place the tassels on the sticks.

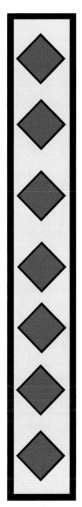

Layout diagram of the bellpull.

Tin Can Vase

What? A crazy quilted vase? It's a great little recycling idea. You will need two cans and the crazy quilting materials of your choice. Use it for dried arrangements by adding some clean pebbles to the bottom or to use with water, add a jar to the vase, putting the water and the flowers in the jar.

The vase shown here is made of two 1-pound coffee cans.

Materials

- 2 identical cans, the size of your choice
- Plastic packaging tape
- Fabric for the foundation (see Step 3 for sizing)
- Fabric scraps for the patches
- Embroidery and embellishment materials
- Fabric for the backing (see Step 3 for sizing)
- Cording

Instructions

1. Use a can opener to remove the bottom of one of the cans.

2. Stack the bottomless can on top of the other and use plastic packaging tape (or any tape that will hold securely) to hold the cans together. Place additional tape over any sharp edges.

3. Measure the circumference and height of the cans. Cut one piece of foundation fabric and one piece from the backing fabric this size, adding 1" all around.

4. Crazy patch the foundation using the method of your choice. Embroider and embellish as desired.

5. Sew the backing fabric and crazy quilted piece at the top and bottom, right sides together.

6. Turn it right-side out and press. Press one of the side edges under.

7. Wrap the piece around the cans and pin.

8. Slipstitch the piece in place.

9. Wrap the cording around the top of the cans and tie in a bow.

The One-Layer Topstitch Appliqué Method

This is similar to Topstitch Appliqué, but has no foundation, and the patch edges are left unfinished. Use heavier fabrics such as denim, wool and some decorator fabrics, especially those that ravel easily. Along with the one-layer throw on page 46, you can make skirts, jackets and vests with this method.

1. Cut a patch-sized piece of fabric with one edge rounded.

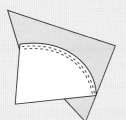

2. Lay the rounded edge onto a second piece of fabric. Sew a seam about ½" in, then another about ⅛" to ¼" in from the edge.

3. Turn the piece over to the wrong side and trim the second fabric to leave a raw edge the same width as the right side.

4. Continue to add patches in the same way. You can mix rounded edges with straight ones for variety. Always turn the piece over and trim the back—then the piece will be reversible.

5. Wash the piece to help the raw edges to fray. Trim any long threads that come loose.

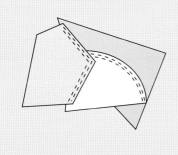

For a variation, apply trims while sewing the patches in place as demonstrated in this detail of the Hope Chest Cover on page 54.

Denim-Lined Quilted Basket

Stuff this basket with a knitting or quilting project and carry it anywhere. The nice thing about a fabric basket is that it can be stuffed into places like behind the seat of a car. Crunch it up and stuff it into the closet when you don't need it!

Materials

- Large piece of paper
- Pencil
- Scissors
- ¼ yd. lengths of 100 percent cotton quilting fabrics in 8 different colors
- 2 yd. batting
- 2 yd. plain cotton fabric for the backing
- Quilting thread
- Several pairs of worn-out blue jeans
- Pearl cotton for tying, size 8
- Heavy thread
- Chenille or other heavy needle
- Used narrow leather belt
- Hammer
- Nail
- Wooden block
- Three 1" brass rings

(½" seam allowance)

Patch the Outer Layer

1. Using the large piece of paper, pencil and scissors, make a 17" circle pattern for the bottom of the basket.

2. Work Confetti Piecing to make a piece the size of the circle.

3. For the basket sides, Confetti piece a rectangle 17½" x 49".

4. Cut out batting and backing fabric the same sizes as both Confetti pieces.
Note: To make a different size or to find the length to make the side piece, measure around the outer edge of the circle. Add a little extra for seam allowance.

TOOLBOX

✓ Confetti Piecing, page 10
✓ The One-Layer Topstitch Appliqué Method, page 41
✓ Machine Quilting, page 141
✓ Tie the Quilt, page 143
✓ Circle Pattern, page 139

Assemble the Bottom and Sides

1. Layer the pieces in the following order: backing fabric (right side down), batting, Confetti piece (right side up) for each section (top and sides).

2. Quilt the pieces by machine using the quilting pattern of your choice.

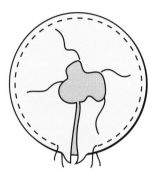

3. With right sides together, first pin, then sew the side piece to the basket bottom. Start and end the stitching about 2" from the ends of the side piece. Check that the side piece will come together with ½" seam allowance. Make any necessary adjustments.

4. Sew the side seam and finish the seam with bias binding or zigzagging. Complete the bottom seam. Finish this seam same as for side seam. Set aside.

Patch the Inner Layer

1. Cut apart the jeans, discarding seams, zipper sections and any areas too worn to use.

2. Using the One-Layer Topstitch Appliqué method, make a bottom and side piece using the same measurements as above.

Assemble the Two Layers

1. Sew the bottom and side piece together, following the instructions in Steps 3 and 4 in the Assemble the Bottom and Sides section.

2. Place the liner inside the quilted basket with wrong sides together, aligning the side seams.

3. Pin the upper edges together. Machine baste ½" from the edge, then zigzag the raw edges together.

4. Thread a sturdy hand sewing needle with doubled heavy-duty thread.

5. Roll the upper edge ½" to the outside, then ½" again.

6. Slipstitch the rolled edge in place just over the basting so the basting doesn't show.

7. Tie the layers using doubled pearl cotton, making the ties on the inside of the basket.

8. Machine wash the basket. Dry by hanging or machine.

9. Trim away any denim threads that have come loose leaving a light fringe on each seam.

Make and Attach the Handles

1. To make the handles, cut the leather belt in half.

2. Fold about 1½" of each leather piece over a brass ring.

3. To stitch the leather, first make nail holes through it, then stitch by hand using heavy-duty thread and a sturdy needle. Work over the beginning of the thread instead of knotting it, and work the final end under the stitching a few times to secure.

4. Sew three brass rings onto the belt pieces and use the belt's buckle for the fourth.

5. Sew the brass rings and the buckle to the basket, placing them 2" down from the top and placing the two ends of each handle 2¾" apart.

Crazy Leather Frame

Yes, you can crazy quilt with leather! I used it to frame a small photo in grand Western style. Collect an assortment of colors in garment-weight leather, then piece them together, as described below.

Materials

- Photocopier
- Heavy paper
- Scissors
- Assorted leather scraps
- Sewing thread
- Needle
- Beeswax
- Waxed linen thread in black
- Chenille needle, size 18
- If needed: small finishing nail, hammer, block of wood
- Foam core, same size as pattern
- 8" x 8½" piece of muslin
- 8" x 8½" piece of brown cotton velveteen
- White glue
- Photo
- 5" x 5½" piece of mat board or acid-free cardboard

TOOLBOX

✓ Feather Stitch, page 140

Patch the Leather

1. Photocopy the pattern onto the heaviest paper the copier will allow.

2. Cut one patch from the pattern at a time.

3. Trace around the cut out piece onto the leather and cut out the leather patch. As each piece is cut, place it in its correct place on a flat surface so that it will not be disturbed.

4. Thread the sewing needle with a doubled length of sewing thread and wax it.

5. Hold two adjoining leather patches together and hand sew through the edges of the back of the patches. Use tiny stitches that will not show on the front. Repeat to join all of the pieces.

6. Thread the chenille needle with the waxed linen thread. Knot the end in a large enough knot that will not slip through.

7. Work a row of single feather stitch along each seam. If the leather is too thick to push the needle through, pound holes for the stitches using the hammer and nail, with the wooden block underneath.

Assemble the Frame

1. Cut the foam core to the size of the outer edge of the pattern. Cut out the inner rectangle.

2. Trim off the outer corners of the muslin.

3. Lay the foam core on the muslin and overlap the edges onto the back of the foam core.

4. Cut the inner rectangle into an X shape.

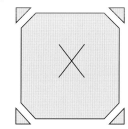

Trim the outer corners and cut an X shape in the inner rectangle.

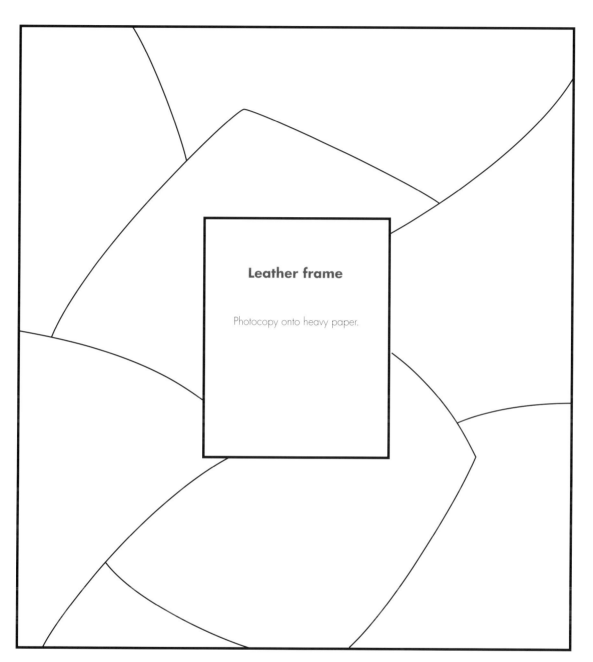

Leather frame

Photocopy onto heavy paper.

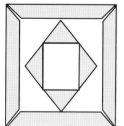

5. Fold the edges over the foam core and glue. Allow the glue to dry.

6. Trim and glue the velveteen in the same manner as the muslin, placing it over the muslin.

Note: When glueing, do not place glue along the edge where the leather piece will be stitched to the fabrics. The glue will stiffen the fabric and make it difficult to stitch.

7. When the glue is completely dry, place the leather piece on the front of the frame. Hand stitch it to the layers of fabric, making tiny stitches into the backs of the leather only.

8. Glue or tape the photo to the back of the frame.

9. Cover the back with the piece of mat board and glue the mat in place.

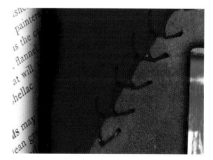

Stitch the leather to the velveteen along the edges.

Lite 'N Airy Southwest Throw

One-Layer Topstitch Appliqué makes great lightweight afghans! Collect some coarsely woven cotton or wool decorator fabrics that ravel easily and have substantial threads in both warp and weft. Set aside one of the fabrics to make fringe and tassels for the edging.

Finished size: 38" square, not including the fringe.

Materials

- ¼ yd. lengths of 6 or more decorator fabrics in shades of sand, adobe and sage
- ½ yd. decorator fabric for the fringe
- Sewing thread in a blending color

(½" seam allowance)

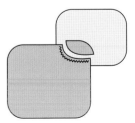

Make the Patches

1. Begin by cutting rectangular patches out of the decorator fabrics (4" to 6" across). Round the corners.

2. Overlap one patch onto another and sew, using a close zigzag stitch about ½" in from the edge of the upper patch.

3. Flip the piece over and trim away the excess from the bottom patch, leaving about ½".

TOOLBOX

✓ The One-Layer Topstitch Appliqué Method, page 41   ✓ A Basic Tassel, page 142

4. Continue to add patches in this way until the afghan is the size desired.

5. Square up the afghan and trim all edges evenly. Round the corners.

Make the Fringe

(To make thicker fringe, use a double layer of the decorator fabric.)

1. At one end of the decorator fabric reserved for the fringe, pull out threads until one thread pulls out continuously from one side to the other. Trim all ends evenly.

2. Cut a strip of the decorator fabric 4" wide. Remove the selvedges.

3. About ½" from one edge, sew a close, narrow zigzag stitch to lock the threads in place. Sew a second row if the first is not adequate.

4. Sew a wide zigzag stitch along the edge.

5. Remove the threads to make the fringe, up to 1" from the top.

6. Hang the removed threads over the back of a chair to keep them from tangling. Make sections of fringe until there are enough to go around the afghan.

Sew the Fringe to the Afghan

1. Fold and press the seam allowance of the outer edge of the afghan to the front.

2. Tuck the header of the fringe under the fold and machine baste all around.

3. Fold the fringe outward. Topstitch and edge stitch along the top of the fringe and through the folded edge of the afghan.

Make and Attach the Tassels

1. Make each tassel out of six of the strands removed from the fringe, follow the basic tassel instructions.

2. Place one at each corner and distribute the others evenly around the afghan. Sew them by hand to the back of the fringe header.

3. To bring each tassel to the front, pull it forward, then tie two strands of the fringe into a square knot behind the tassel.

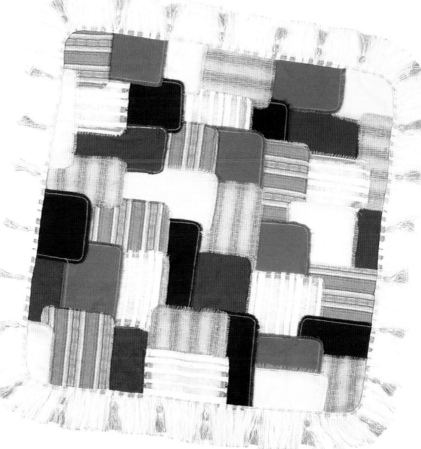

Beaded Table Runner

This beaded runner is simply made of bandings that are fastened together with beading. A beaded fringe completes the ends.

The bandings finish to 3" wide. Make the piece to the length needed for your table. For a wider runner, add bandings to the width.

Finished size: approximately 6" x 45"

Materials

- Small pieces of 6 or more decorator fabrics in shades of sand, adobe and sage
- Fabric for the backing
- 4mm beads
- Seed beads, size 6
- Seed beads, size 11
- Nylon beading thread

(½" seam allowance)

TOOLBOX

✓ The One-Layer Topstitch Appliqué Method, page 41
✓ Looped Fringe, page 138
✓ Backing, page 138

Make the Two Bandings

1. Using the decorator fabrics and the One-layer Topstitch Appliqué method, make two pieces, each 4" wide by the length desired. Be sure to add seam allowances to the ends.

2. Cut two pieces of backing fabric using the same measurements.

3. Place one backing piece and one banding right sides together and sew around, leaving an opening to turn.

4. Turn, press and slipstitch the opening closed. Repeat for the second banding.

Join the Bandings

1. Join the bandings using the size 6 seed beads. Fasten on beading thread at the end of one banding. Place a bead on the thread and take a stitch about ¼" long in the second banding. Add another bead and take a stitch in the first banding. Continue adding beads at ¼" intervals.

2. Sew seed beads at ¼" intervals on the outer edges of the runner.

3. At the ends of the runner, make looped fringe, making each loop 1" long out of size 11 seed beads (string on 2" of beads), and using the 4mm beads as the header beads.

Coiled Confetti Basket

If you are a basket lover like me, you'll want to make a bunch of these. Make them any size you want! A small basket is perfect to hold a few items of jewelry. A larger one can hold your threads or yarns for a needlework project. Instructions are for the larger basket with ribbonworked florals. You can add decorations, such as the cordings and gathered flowers shown here.

Vary the quantities of the materials to make your basket in the size of your choice. For the core material, you can use a soft, round braided rope if that is easier to find. If you substitute a rope or core of a different size, change the width of the Confetti banding to fit around it.

Make the Banding

1. Work Confetti Piecing to make a strip of banding 12 yd. x 2¼" wide.

2. Cut 2¼" wide bias strips of muslin and piece them together to make a piece 12 yards long.

3. Place the muslin on the back of the Confetti-pieced banding and machine sew about ⅛" from one long edge.

4. Press under the same edge ¼".

Materials

- 12 yd. welting or core material, ⅜" diameter
- ¼ yd. lengths of 100 percent cotton quilting fabrics in 8 different colors
- 1 yd. muslin
- Upholstery thread or other heavy thread
- Chenille needle or other heavy needle
- Materials as desired for embellishment

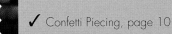

TOOLBOX

✓ Confetti Piecing, page 10   ✓ Slipstitching, page 142

Wrap the Cord with the Banding

1. Starting at one end of the rope, wrap the sewn strip over the rope beginning with the raw edge, and pin it in place.

2. Slipstitch along the folded edge to secure.

3. To finish the ends, pull the rope out of the sewn strip just a short way, and trim it so it will be about ½" shorter than the fabric strip. Fold in the fabric and stitch neatly.

Coil the Basket

1. Begin coiling the basket using the heavy thread and needle, stitching the coils together. Stitch into the slipstitched seam, then into the previously sewn coil. Shape the basket as you stitch. To reinforce the stitching, it may be necessary to follow along with a second row of stitching near to the first.

2. Decorate the basket if you like. You can add ribbonworked florals (see the Piano Shawl on page 35), beading, embroidery, fringes or leather handles.

Shape the basket over a bowl while sewing.

Calendar Pockets

Materials

- ¼ yd. lengths of 100 percent cotton quilting fabrics in 8 different colors
- ½ yd. denim or other sturdy fabric
- ½ yd. fabric for the backing
- ½ yd. batting
- Quilting thread in the color of your choice*
- Cotton fabric for the bias binding
- Trims as desired such as eyelet laces, self-made cordings and buttons
- 4 bone rings
- Materials to make two tassels
- Calendar
- 24½" wooden stick with desired finish
- 6 cup hooks

*Used in this project: YLI Quilting Thread

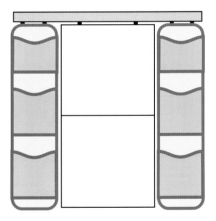

Layout diagram for the calendar pocket set-up.

The calendar and pockets are hanging from a wooden stick, which here is covered by a piece of weathered wood for decoration. The pockets are designed to fit a 12" x 23" calendar.

These pockets are super handy because you can use them to hold your bills and calendar at the same time, so you can see when to pay them! The pockets can hold some pens and a checkbook, too. Use the pockets for a calculator, checkbook, address book, pads of paper for shopping lists, your grocery coupons, etc. Make one for household use and another for the home (or away) office.

TOOLBOX

✓ Confetti Piecing, page 10
✓ Bias Strips and Bias Bindings, pages 138-139
✓ Machine Quilting, page 141
✓ Gathering, page 141

Make the Pocket Panels

1. Cut two pieces 6" x 23" out of both the denim and backing fabrics.

2. Place a backing on the back of each denim piece and handle the two as one.

3. Work Confetti Piecing to make enough to cut out the following pockets: cut two pockets each 6" x 5". Cut four pockets each 6" x 6".

4. Cut corresponding pieces from both the batting and the backing fabric.

5. Layer the pockets in the following order: Confetti Piecing on top, batting, then backing. Pin the layers and baste if desired.

6. Quilt each pocket in the freeform pattern of your choice using the colored quilting thread. If desired, shape the upper edges of the pockets as shown.

7. Gather eyelet lace and pin to the upper edge of each pocket.

8. Cut the fabric for the bias binding into strips 2⅛" wide to make 7½ yards of bias binding.

9. Make the bias binding.

10. Apply bias binding to the upper and lower edges of each pocket.

11. Add trims such as sewn-on cordings and buttons to each pocket.

12. Arrange the pockets on the two denim pieces, having a smaller pocket at the top followed by two larger pockets. Pin. Cut the corners of the denim pieces rounded if desired.

13. Apply bias binding all around each denim pocket piece.

14. Sew two bone rings to the upper edge of the back of each piece. If desired, make and add a tassel to the bottom of each.

Assemble the Calendar Center

1. Punch two holes through the top edge of the calendar.

2. Lay the stick on a flat surface and arrange calendar and pockets just beneath it.

3. Determine placements of the cup hooks. Screw in two for each pocket piece and two for the calendar.

4. Fasten the stick to the wall using screws and drywall anchors, or by the method of your choice.

Hope Chest Cover

Here is a way to make a loose, draping cover for a piece of furniture which, by itself, will shift around and end up on the floor. The solution is to make two pieces. First, make a padded cover that is securely fastened to the furniture. Second, make the draped cover and fasten it to the padded one.

This idea may also be adapted for other types of furniture. In that case, decide how best to secure the padded cover so it stays in place. This hope chest cover uses a sleeve and ties. *Optional:* Add a really fancy decorator tassel.

Materials

For the padded cover
- Newspaper for the pattern
- Scissors
- Outer fabric such as a smooth cotton, enough for the front, back and a sleeve
- Cotton fabric for the bias binding
- Layers of quilt batting for padding
- Pearl cotton for tying
- Snap fasteners or hook and loop tape

For the draped cover
- Newspaper
- Tape
- Scissors
- Scraps of denim and additional fabrics as desired
- Trims such as self-made cordings, braids, cotton laces and eyelet laces
- Fabric for the backing
- Pearl cotton for tying
- Tasseled trim for the edging

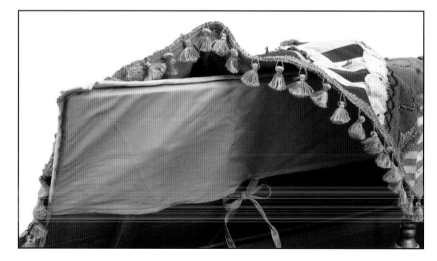

TOOLBOX

✓ The One-Layer Topstitch Appliqué Method, page 41

✓ Bias Strips and Bias Bindings, pages 138-139

✓ Tie the Quilt, page 143
✓ Tassels, pages 142-143
✓ Paper Patterns, page 141

Make the Padded Cover

1. Make a newspaper pattern to fit the top of the piece of furniture.

2. Using the newspaper pattern, cut one piece of fabric for the front and one for the back, making each about 1" larger all around.

3. Cut the batting the same size as the newspaper pattern.

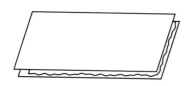

4. Stack the fabric and batting, making a sandwich with the batting in the middle. Pin.

5. Tie the layers.

6. Baste around the edges. Trim the piece to the size of the pattern or just a bit larger.

Make the Sleeve

1. Make the sleeve the same width as the pattern. Choose how deep to make it and add a seam allowance.

2. Hem one long edge.

3. Place the sleeve on the wrong side of the padded section and pin.

4. Baste the sleeve to the padded cover.

5. Determine the number of ties you will need (I used four) and the length (you can make them longer, then cut them to size later). For each tie, cut a lengthwise strip of fabric 2" wide.

6. Fold the side edges of the tie to the center. Fold again along the center.

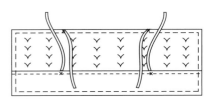

7. Sew along the edges.

8. Sew two ties to the side of the hemmed edge of the sleeve.

9. Pin the remaining two to the corresponding location on the wrong side of the padded piece.

10. Make a bias binding and bind the entire outer edge.

11. Place the cover on the furniture and tie in place.

Make the Draped Cover

1. Make a newspaper pattern the size and shape desired. The draped cover should hang down over the sides of the furniture. You may need to tape sheets of newspaper together to do this. Remember, it does not have to be the same shape as the padded cover, as shown above.

2. Use the One-Layer Topstitch Appliqué method to piece the denim scraps and other fabrics, making the piece the same size as the paper pattern.

3. Add additional decoration such as:
- Gather eyelet lace into flowers. Make the centers by covering a plastic button with fabric, or roll fringed fabric and stitch on.
- Cut squares of denim, sew them on, then ravel the edges.
- Sew self-made cordings into spirals and other shapes, allowing the ends to ravel.

4. Cut the backing fabric the same size as the cover.

5. Place the fabric on the back of the patched piece. Zigzag around the edges.

6. Sew tasseled trim on top of the zigzagging.

7. Tie the cover using pearl cotton.

8. Sew on snap fasteners or hook and loop tape to fasten the draped cover to the padded cover.

Chapter 3

Victorian adVenture!

Sweet Heart

Patch this heart in the Antique Method. Include smidgens of fine laces, handmade cordings, a touch of silk ribbon embroidery, eyelet lace and some beads. Before assembling the heart, sew the ends and gather a 25" length of 1¾" wide eyelet lace and pin it to the crazy patched heart (see Backing). Finish by sewing on a tassel.

TOOLBOX

✓ The Antique Method of Crazy Quilting, page 12

✓ Backing, page 138

✓ A Basic Tassel, page 142

✓ Cordings, page 139

✓ Gathering, page 141

✓ Heart Pattern, page 15

Victorian Fans Quilt with Shirred Border

Materials

- 1½ yd. 100 percent cotton velveteen fabric
- 2 yd. muslin fabric
- Heavy-duty thread
- Photocopier or tracing paper
- Paper
- Scissors for cutting paper
- Silk and cotton fabrics for the fans
- Assorted fabric scraps including silks for crazy patches
- Pearl cotton for embroidery on the fans, size 8
- Hand-dyed silk threads, silk ribbons, and other threads of your choice for embroidery*
- Embellishments of your choice including laces, braids, trims and cordings
- ½ yd. cotton sateen or other fabric for sashings
- 3½ yd. plain cotton fabric for the backing and binding in a color to match the border
- Threads for tying
- Silk ribbon for the bows, 1" wide (optional)

*Used in this project: Vikki Clayon's hand-dyed silk threads and ribbons

Begin by gathering a selection of fabrics, threads and trims.

In grand Victorian style, this quilt is an elegant throw or wallhanging. Royal blue velveteen makes a luxurious fan background and shirred border. As intricate as it looks, it is not a huge project! All of the crazy quilting is confined to four blocks, and the fans are quickly, easily and accurately pieced using the paper piecing method.

Choose your own color scheme, embroidery threads and favorite methods of embellishment to make this quilt your own.

TOOLBOX

✓ The Antique Method of Crazy Quilting, page 12

✓ Paper Piecing of Fans, page 141

✓ Outline Stitch, page 140

✓ Coral Stitch, page 140

✓ Bias Strips and Bias Bindings, pages 138-139

✓ Rod Pocket, page 142

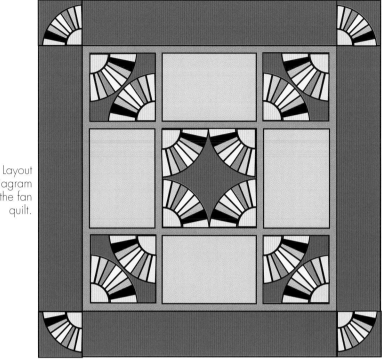

Layout diagram of the fan quilt.

Make the Fans

(½" seam allowances)

1. Make 16 photocopies of the fan pattern (or make 16 tracings onto artist tracing paper).

2. Using the appropriate cutting lines, cut the the following number of patterns:
- Four patterns for 6" blocks
- Eight patterns for 9" blocks
- Four patterns for 13" blocks

3. Follow instructions for the Paper Piecing of Fans. Seam allowances are not included in the pattern, so be sure to add these to the outer edges as you piece the fans.

Make the Velveteen Blocks

1. From the velveteen fabric:
- Cut one center block 14" square.
- Cut four blocks each 10" square.
- Cut four corner blocks each 7" square.

2. From the muslin:
- Cut one 14" square for the center block.
- Cut four 10" square blocks.
- Cut four 7" squares for the corner blocks.

3. Back each velveteen block with muslin and handle the two as one. *Note:* It looks best to have the nap of the velveteen running in the same direction for all of the blocks when they are sewn into the quilt. When the nap runs upward, the velveteen has a deep, rich look to it. To do this, arrange the blocks as they will be in the quilt, then place the fans on them. See the quilt diagram for fan placements.

Assemble the Fan and Velveteen Blocks

1. Place the four largest fans onto the 14" velveteen center block. Pin carefully.

2. Place one small fan on each of the 7" blocks. Pin carefully.

3. Place two of the remaining fans on each of the four 10" blocks. Pin carefully.

4. Slipstitch along the curved top of each fan through all layers.

5. Open out each fan and trim away the velveteen from under the fan (but not the muslin), leaving a seam allowance of ¼" to ½".

6. Baste around each block.

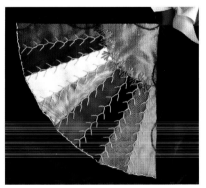

7. Finish the fans by working the feather stitch along the blades and the coral stitch along the tops using size 8 pearl cotton, as shown.

8. Embroider along the fan centers.

Patch the Blocks

1. Cut four blocks of muslin each 10" x 14".

2. Patch each of the blocks using the assorted fabric scraps in the Antique Method.

3. Embellish and embroider as desired.

Make the Borders

1. Cut four pieces of muslin 7" x 37".

2. Cut four pieces of velveteen each 7" x 54".

3. Gather the velveteen pieces and hand or machine baste along each long edge using heavy-duty thread. Draw up the thread until the velveteen piece is the same length as the muslin piece.

4. Adjust the gathers evenly and pin the velveteen to the muslin.

5. Baste, then zigzag around all the edges of the border to prevent ravelling.

Assemble the Quilt

1. Place the completed blocks in order on the floor or other large surface.

2. Cut 1" wide sashings and sew them between blocks to make three columns of three blocks each. Press seams as each is sewn.

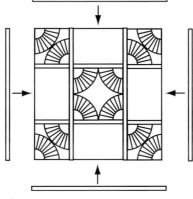

3. Cut two long sashings and join the columns.

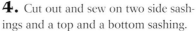

4. Cut out and sew on two side sashings and a top and a bottom sashing.

5. Sew on two side borders.

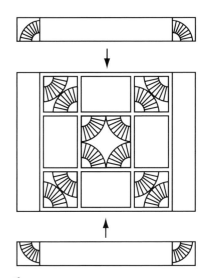

6. Sew a corner block to each end of the two remaining borders and sew them onto the quilt.

7. Embroider a meandering outline stitch along the edges of the sashings and the border (as shown in the photo).

8. Cut and sew the backing fabric to make a piece the same size as the quilt.

9. Place it on the back of the quilt. Pin.

10. Cut bias bindings 2⅛" wide and apply it to the sides, top and bottom of the quilt, finishing the edges neatly.

11. Tie the quilt. If desired, sew silk bows at the corners of the blocks.

12. Add a rod pocket if the quilt is a wallhanging.

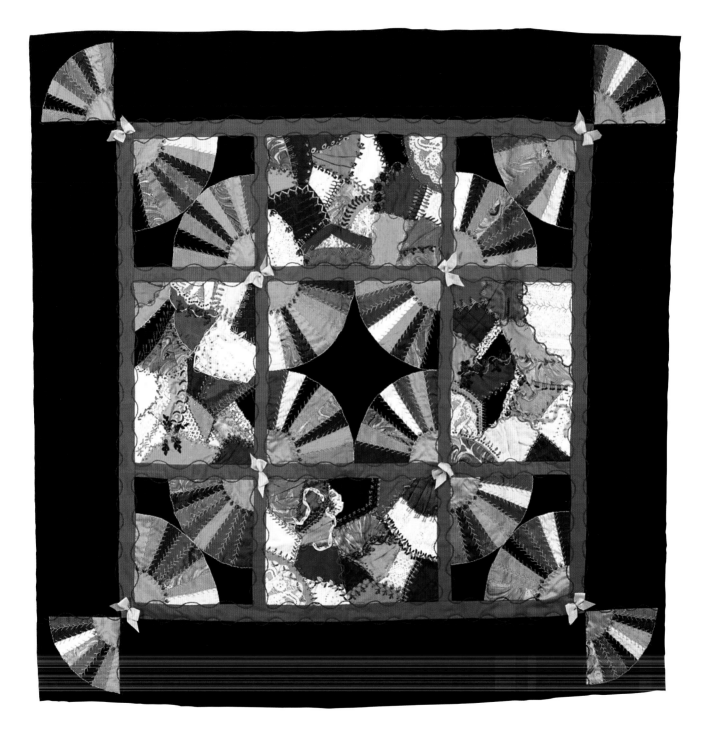

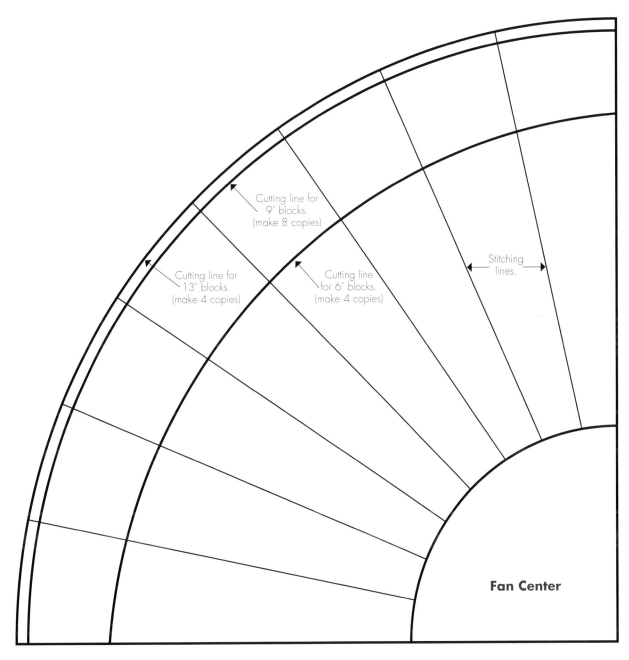

Cutting line for
9" blocks.
(make 8 copies)

Cutting line for
13" blocks.
(make 4 copies)

Cutting line
for 6" blocks.
(make 4 copies)

Stitching
lines.

Fan Center

Fan

Fan Bellpull

Set the fans on their sides for this bellpull. The edges of the bellpull are gathered onto cording to match the shirring of the quilt.

Materials

- ¼ yd. muslin for the foundation
- Fabric scraps for the patches and fans
- Rayon threads in several colors*
- 2½ yd. cotton filler cord
- 4 yd. bias-cut cotton velveteen strips, a width that will go around the filler cord plus seam allowances
- ¼ yd. plain cotton fabric for the backing
- Large Victorian-style tassel
- Bone ring

*Used in this project: YLI Pearl Crown Rayon threads

(½" seam allowance)

TOOLBOX

✓ The Antique Method of Crazy Quilting, page 12

✓ Fan Pattern, page 61
✓ Paper Piecing of Fans, page 141

✓ Tassels, pages 142-143

Layout diagram of the bellpull.

Patch the Fans

1. Make two fans using the cutting line for the 6" blocks on page 61.

2. Follow instructions for the Paper Piecing of Fans. Seam allowances are not included in the pattern, so be sure to add these to the outer edges as you piece the fans. (Make the fan centers slightly smaller than the pattern given. When the fan is placed onto the bellpull, cut the blades to size so the fan fits the width of the bellpull.)

3. Cut the muslin and backing fabric each 5½" x 27".

4. Patch the muslin in the Antique Method.

5. Embroider the patched piece using the rayon threads.

6. Sew one fan to each end of the bellpull as shown in the diagram.

7. Embroider the fans.

Make and Attach the Gathered Cording

1. Measure around the bellpull and cut the filler cord this length.

2. With a zipper foot on the machine, sew the bias-cut velveteen onto the filler cord, stitching next to the cord, but taking care to not catch the cord in the stitching. Secure the beginning end with pins or by stitching. As you sew, pull on the filler cord to push the velveteen toward the beginning so it gathers. End so the velveteen is about ½" longer than the cording. Secure the end with a few stitches.

3. With right sides together, sew the ruched velveteen cording all around the bellpull, beginning and ending at the bottom.

4. To finish the cording ends, unsecure them and fold and stitch the velveteen so all raw edges are finished.

Finish the Bellpull

1. Press under the seam allowance of the backing and pin it to the back of the bellpull.

2. Slipstitch the backing to the seam line of the gathered edging.

3. Sew a bone ring to the upper back.

4. Sew a tassel to the bottom.

Heart Pillow

Make several of these and scatter them on a bed or a couch. They also make great gifts! Use the same mix of fabrics and trims for the Fleece Blanket on page 74. Add some old lace and a cotton or rayon motif. This pillow is made with a gusset to give it a box-like shape.

Materials

- 15" x 13" piece of paper
- Pencil
- Scissors
- 15" x 16" piece of foundation fabric
- Scraps of cotton decorator fabrics in an assortment of textures, solids and muted prints in burgundy, rose, soft grey, beige and cream
- Cotton laces, old and new, natural and white
- Various sizes of rayon cordings in gold, burgundy and grey
- Rayon threads in burgundy, dark green, gold, black and beige*
- ½ yd. cotton decorator fabric for the backing
- ¼ yd. velveteen for the gusset
- 2¾ yd. bias strips of decorator fabric for the welting
- 2¾ yd. cotton filler cord for the welting
- ¾ yd. muslin or other fabric for the pillow insert and gusset
- Stuffing

*Used in this project: YLI Pearl Crown Rayon threads

(¼" seam allowance)

TOOLBOX

✓ The Antique Method of Crazy Quilting, page 12

✓ Welting, page 143

Patch the Heart

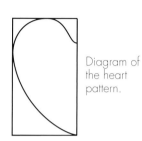

Diagram of the heart pattern.

1. To make a heart pattern, fold the 15" x 13" sheet of paper in half and sketch half of a heart shape. Cut out the heart (see diagram).

2. Use the pattern to cut one heart from the foundation fabric and backing fabric, and two from the muslin, adding ¼" seam allowance all around each.

3. Using the Antique Method of crazy patching, patch the foundation adding laces into some of the seams, if desired.

4. Hand stitch cordings along some of the patch edges.

5. Embroider using the rayon threads and embroidery stitches of your choice.

6. Make the welting.

7. Baste the welting to the pillow top.

8. Baste another piece to the pillow back.

Decorator fabrics were collected for this and several projects following.

Assemble the Pillow

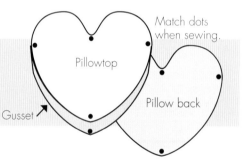

Note: To get the gusset to go on evenly, first sew one edge of the gusset to the pillow top. Establish some points that match on both pillow top and backing, and mark the same points on the gusset. Align these when the backing is sewn on.

1. Cut a piece of muslin for the gusset 2½" x the circumference of the paper pattern plus seam allowances, piecing fabric if necessary.

2. Pepare a piece of velveteen 2½" wide x 1½ times the length of the muslin.

3. Zigzag the edges to prevent ravelling.

4. Gather the long edges until it is the same length as the muslin. Place the velveteen piece onto the muslin, adjust gathers if necessary, and baste the two together.

5. Sew the short ends of the gusset together to make one continuous piece.

6. With right sides together, pin, then sew one long edge of the gusset to the pillow top.

7. Pin, then sew the other long edge of the gusset to the pillow back, leaving an opening to turn.

8. Trim, turn and press.

9. Stuff the pillow, taking care to retain its boxy shape.

10. Slipstitch the opening closed.

The Heirloom Method of Crazy Quilting

This is another variation of Topstitch Appliqué, similar to the One-Layer method given in the previous chapter. Join laces and sheer batiste fabric to make lacy curtains and other projects. It is simple, and all of the edges are finished, which makes the projects two-sided. You will need stabilizer and a sewing machine that has a zigzag stitch. Stabilizer can be almost any commercial product, plain paper or artist's tracing paper. Find the procedure that works the best for you!

Note: Use an embroidery foot. Set the machine to a short and narrow zigzag, but not too short because you want the sewing to move along. The width of the stitch should be the same as the amount of seam allowance (same as the fabric edging of the entredeux).

If your sewing machine functions as most do, the zigzagging will pull most of the seams into a rounded shape. This is alright and actually desirable since it more closely resembles a hand-rolled edge.

1. Begin by preparing the patch fabrics. It is easier to create these as large pieces that can be cut into patches rather than making them patch-sized. For example, take ½ yard of batiste fabric and set laces into it. On another piece, work pintucks, and so on.

2. Cut a patch-sized piece of one of the prepared fabrics, making one edge rounded.

3. Lay the rounded edge onto a second piece of prepared fabric. Zigzag along the raw edge through both layers.

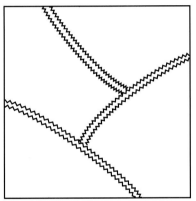

4. Sew a second zigzag seam about ⅜" in from the first.

5. Flip the piece over and trim the second fabric as close as you can to the stitching. All edges are then finished.

6. Continue to add patches in the same way. Always trim the back neatly so no excess fabric remains. Add patches until the piece is the size needed.

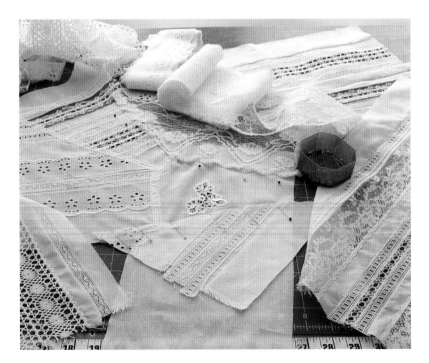

Heirloom Sewing Techniques

Materials

- 100 percent cotton batiste fabric
- Stabilizer
- Entredeux
- Cotton sewing thread
- Cotton laces
- Lace motifs

Heirloom sewing involves joining trims and laces to batiste fabric creating an effect that is both elegant and delicate-looking.

The following techniques are my adaptation of heirloom sewing techniques. Normally, the fabric edging the holes of the entredeux is trimmed away and the zigzag stitching plunks into the holes of two trims, thus joining them. (Entredeux is a narrow trim that is used to join fabrics or laces to each other.) I have opted instead to retain the fabric edge as a seam allowance. You can try both methods and see which you prefer. Either method can be used.

Variations

Joining entredeux to fabric or another entredeux

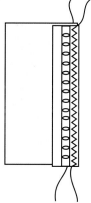

With right sides together, zigzag along the fabric edging, but not into the entredeux itself.

Joining lace to fabric or entredeux

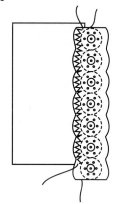

With right sides up, lap the edge of the lace onto the fabric edge of the entredeux or onto the edge of the fabric. Zigzag stitch the two together.

Joining two laces

With right sides up, overlap one edge onto the other and zigzag (same as above).

Making puffing and joining it to entredeux

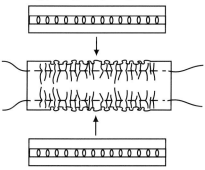

Cut a piece of batiste 2" wide by twice the length of a piece of entredeux. Machine baste along each long edge. Pull up to gather, fitting the puffing to the entredeux. Place the two right sides together and adjust the gathers evenly. Zigzag the seam allowances together.

Setting lace motifs into fabric

With right sides up, place motif on the fabric and carefully zigzag all around. Turn the piece over and very carefully trim away the fabric behind the motif, trimming as close to the stitching as possible.

Making tucks

Cut a piece of batiste fabric the length desired. Press evenly spaced creases (one crease for each tuck). Sew along the edge of each crease using a straight stitch.

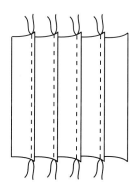

Crazy Lace Curtain

Yardages of laces and fabric will depend on the size of the curtain and your usage of the materials. Either buy more materials than you think you will need, or work up a sample piece and try to determine what the total yardages will come to.

Be as ambitious as you want! Make a panel for a large window or make a small curtain for a door window. Make a crazy quilted tieback to use with your curtain.

Materials

- 8 to 10 different cotton laces and entredeux
- 100 percent cotton batiste fabric
- Stabilizer
- Wide eyelet lace 1½ times the width of the finished curtain

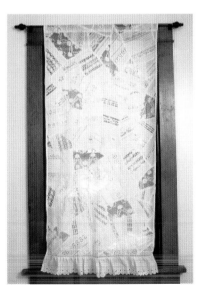

TOOLBOX

✓ The Heirloom Method of Crazy Quilting, page 66
✓ Rod Pocket, page 142

Determine the Size of the Curtain

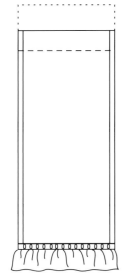

Sizing the curtain.

1. Make the panel wide enough to gather slightly on the curtain rod.

2. Add 2½" to the length for the rod pocket at the top. Also, figure in the length of the eyelet lace ruffle at the bottom.

Patch the Curtain

1. Follow instructions for the Heirloom Method to make a piece the size needed for your curtain.

2. Sew entredeux to the bottom edge of the curtain.

3. Machine baste along the raw edge of the eyelet lace, then gather it to fit the curtain.

4. With right sides together, sew the eyelet to the entredeux.

Finish the Curtain

1. Cut bias strips of batiste fabric 2⅛" wide.

2. Using ½" seam allowance, bind the side edges of the curtain.

3. Finish the bottom ends by folding the bias neatly and stitching.

4. Fold the top of the curtain ½" to the back and press.

5. Fold again to make a 2" rod pocket. Stitch across the folded edge.

A Basic Tieback

Make a crazy quilted tieback for the lace curtain. This is a basic tieback, so you can adjust it to fit most curtain styles. Make it to fit with any décor from the living room to the kitchen to the bedroom.

(½" seam allowance)

1. Cut a piece of foundation fabric 4" x 19".

2. Using the Antique Method of crazy patching, crazy patch the foundation piece, adding laces into some of the seams (optional).

3. Hand stitch cordings along some of the patch edges.

4. Embroider using rayon threads and the embroidery stitches of your choice.

5. Cut a piece of backing fabric the same size.

6. Sew the backing to the tieback right sides together, leaving an opening to turn.

7. Trim the seams, turn and press.

8. Sew cording all around the tieback, concealing the ends in the opening.

9. Slipstitch the opening closed.

10. Sew a bone ring to each end.

TOOLBOX

✓ The Antique Method of Crazy Quilting, page 12   ✓ Backing, page 138   ✓ Cordings, page 139

Lace-Edged Pillowcase

Pillowcase edgings are an easy way to add a touch of lacy crazy patch to your décor. These also make elegant gifts!

Materials

- Purchased pillowcase, white
- Pieces of heirloom sewing
- Eyelet lace 1½ times the length of the pillowcase hem

TOOLBOX

✓ The Heirloom Method of Crazy Quilting, page 66   ✓ Gathering, page 141

Patch the Pillowcase Edge

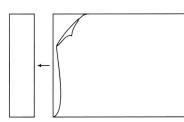

1. Cut off the cuffed end of the pillowcase and rip open the side seam for several inches.

2. Measure the cut end of the pillowcase.

3. Follow instructions for the Heirloom Method to make a piece this length by 4" wide.

Finish the Pillowcase

1. Sew entredeux to each long edge of the band.

2. Machine baste along the raw edge of the eyelet lace, then gather it to fit the band.

3. With right sides together, sew the eyelet to the entredeux on one side of the band.

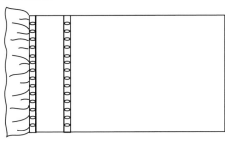

4. Sew the remaining entredeux edge to the pillowcase.

5. Re-sew the side seam of the pillow, continuing onto the band. Finish the seam by zigzagging.

Beaded Lampshade Cover

Materials

- Plain lampshade
- Newspaper
- Scissors
- Pieces of heirloom sewing
- White ribbons
- 1 ⅛" wide bias-cut cotton fabric for the binding
- Decorative ribbon

Optional:
- Beads: clear glass, seed and bugle
- White beading thread
- Beading needle

Make a lace cover for an existing lampshade. This one is finished with a beaded fringe (which is optional). The lampshade cover is fastened by ribbon ties so it can be removed for washing.

TOOLBOX

✓ The Heirloom Method of Crazy Quilting, page 66   ✓ Bias Strips and Biad Binding, pages 138-139

✓ Beaded Fringe, page 138

Patch the Lampshade

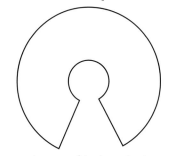

Layout diagram of the lampshade pattern.

1. To make a newspaper pattern the same size as the lampshade, wrap the newspaper around the lampshade and cut it the same shape.

2. Follow instructions for the Heirloom Method to make a piece the same size as the pattern, but add ½" seam allowance to the side edges.

3. Join the side edges and sew them together.

Attach the Ribbon Ties

1. Cutting ribbon to the appropriate lengths, pin three ribbons to the wrong side of the top edge of the cover, evenly spaced.

2. Pin another three to match the locations on the wrong side of the bottom edge.

3. Make bias binding.

4. Bind the top and bottom edges of the cover, catching the ends of the ribbons in the seams.

Finish the Lampshade

1. Make a decorative bow and stitch it to the cover.

2. Optional: Sew beads to the edges of the bias binding, adding a fringe to the bottom if desired.

3. Tie the cover to the lampshade using the ribbons sewn to the inside.

Fancy Fleece Blanket

Materials

- Cream-colored purchased fleece blanket, twin-size
- Muslin for the foundation
- Scraps of cotton decorator fabrics, assortment of textures, solids and muted prints in burgundy, rose, soft grey, beige and cream
- Old and new cotton laces in natural and white
- Various sizes of rayon cordings in gold, burgundy and grey
- Rayon threads in burgundy, dark green, gold, black and beige*
- 1½ yd. cotton fabric for the linings
- 1 yd. white cotton fabric for the bias bindings
- T-square or yardstick

Optional: 3¾ yd. white eyelet lace, or twice the distance to be covered (3½" wide)

*Used in this project: YLI Pearl Crown Rayon threads

Cutting Instructions

From muslin:
- Cut two pieces each 5" x 45".
- Cut two pieces each 5" x 14".

From cotton fabric for the linings:
- Cut two pieces each 5" x 45".
- Cut two pieces each 5" x 14".

(½" seam allowance)

Turn a plain blanket into something fanciful! This blanket is for a twin-size bed. To make other sizes, scale up the design by placing the blanket on the bed and determining how long to make the bandings.

Choose decorator fabrics including some soft, floral prints in muted tones.

Patch the Bandings

1. Using the Antique Method, crazy patch the four lengths of muslin. If desired, add laces into some of the seams.

2. Hand stitch cordings along some of the patch edges.

3. Embroider, using the Pearl Crown Rayon threads and the embroidery stitches of your choice.

Line the Bandings

1. To line each banding, place a lining piece and the banding right sides together. Sew around, leaving an opening to turn.

2. Turn, press and slipstitch the opening closed.

3. Slipstitch the two shorter bandings to the longer ones to form a rectangle.

TOOLBOX

✓ The Antique Method of Crazy Quilting, page 12
✓ Slipstiching, page 142
✓ Embroidery Stitches, page 140
✓ Bias Strips and Bias Binding, pages 138-139

Attach the Banding to the Blanket

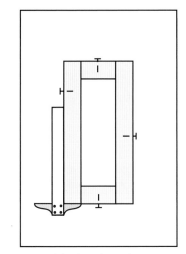

Diagram of the banding placement.

1. Lay the rectangle of bandings on the blanket, centering it carefully, and having it the same distance from the edge on three sides. There will be a wider distance at the upper edge where the blanket will fit over a pillow. Measure in from the edges on all sides, and square up the rectangle using a t-square or yardstick. Pin the rectangle to the blanket.

2. Mark the position of the rectangle (on the outside edge) using pins or chalk.

3. Cut along the markings. Set aside the rectangle and the center portion of the blanket (keeping the bandings pinned to the blanket).

4. Sew the short ends of the eyelet lace together.

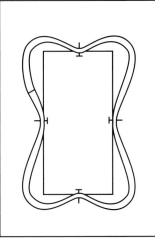

Diagram of the lace placement.

5. Evenly distribute the eyelet lace around the opening in the blanket and place some pins, as shown in the diagram.

6. Between the pins, arrange and pin the eyelet into folds as evenly as you can, adding extra folds to each corner so the eyelet turns the corners smoothly.

7. Cut bias strips 2¼" wide and join them to make one long piece.

8. With right sides together, machine sew the binding to the cut edge of the blanket, sewing the eyelet at the same time.

9. Turn the bias to the back, fold it under and slipstitch it in place, folding neatly at each corner.

10. Cut the cut-away rectangle piece along the inner edges of the bandings. Set aside the bandings. Remove the pins and discard the cut-away part of the blanket (this is the part that was underneath the bandings).

11. Sew a bias strip to each side edge of the (fleece) blanket center. Turn the bias strip to the back and slipstitch.

12. Sew a bias strip to the top and bottom having them overhang by ½" at each end. Slipstitch the bias strip to the back, folding the ends in neatly.

13. Assemble the pieces following the diagram. Pin, then slipstitch having the pieces right-side up.

14. Turn the blanket over and slipstitch again on the back of each seam to secure well.

15. Embroider using the double feather or other stitch along the inner edge of the binding. A way to do this (so you don't have the whole blanket in your lap) is to lay the blanket on a table with a cutting mat underneath.

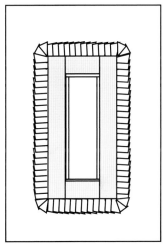

Layout diagram of the fleece blanket.

16. With matching sewing thread, tack the ruffle to the blanket at each corner and a few places in between.

Matching Pillow

Finished size: 18" x 15"

Materials

- ¼ yd. decorator fabric for pillow center and outer borders, a color that coordinates with the fleece blanket
- 1 yd. 100 percent cotton muslin for the foundation and pillow insert
- Scraps of cotton decorator fabrics, assortment of textures, solids and muted prints in burgundy, rose, soft grey, beige and cream
- Various sizes of rayon cordings in gold, burgundy and grey
- Rayon threads in burgundy, dark green, gold, black and beige*
- 3" wide white eyelet lace, twice the circumference of the pillow
- 1 yd. backing fabric
- Stuffing
- Sewing thread

*Used in this project: YLI Crown Rayon threads

Cutting Instructions

From the decorator fabric:
- Cut one 7" x 4" pillow center.
- Cut two 13" x 4" outer borders.
- Cut two 16" x 4" outer borders.

From the muslin:
- Cut two 7" x 4" bandings.
- Cut two 10" x 4" bandings.

From the backing fabric:
- Cut two 19" x 16" pillow insert panels.

(½" seam allowance)

Make a pretty eyelet-decked throw pillow to toss on the bed with the fleece blanket.

TOOLBOX

✓ The Antique Method of Crazy Quilting, page 12

✓ Gathering, page 141
✓ Bandings, page 138

✓ Embroidery Stitches, page 140

Patch the Center Bandings

1. Using the Antique Method, patch the four pieces of muslin, adding laces into some of the seams, if desired.

2. Hand stitch cordings along some of the patch edges.

3. Embroider using the rayon threads and the embroidery stitches of your choice.

Assemble the Pillow Top

1. With right sides together and pressing each seam open, sew the 7" x 4" bandings to the top and bottom of the 7" x 4" pillow center.

2. With right sides together and pressing each seam open, sew the 10" x 4" bandings to the sides of the center piece.

3. With right sides together and pressing each seam open, sew the 13" x 4" outer borders to the top and bottom of the center piece.

4. With right sides together and pressing each seam open, sew the 16" x 4" outer borders to the sides of the center piece.

5. Embroider along the seams.

6. Sew together the short ends of the eyelet lace.

7. Gather the eyelet by machine basting along the seam line, and again within the seam allowance. Draw up on the threads to gather, then pin the lace to the outer edge of the pillow with right sides together. Gather slightly fuller at the corners so they turn smoothly.

Attach the Pillow Back

1. Place the backing fabric and pillow top right sides together.

2. Sew around, leaving an opening to turn. Clip and turn right-side out.

Make the Pillow Insert

1. Place the two pillow insert panels right sides together and sew around, leaving an opening to turn.

2. Turn the pillow right-side out and stuff.

3. Slipstitch the opening closed.

4. Place the insert inside the pillow cover.

5. Slipstitch the opening of the pillow cover closed.

Fringed Table Cover

This is a substantial, upholstery-type tablecloth, suitable for an occasional table. Make it out of decorator fabrics, fabricated patches, fringes, cordings and wide eyelet laces. Add a heavy brush fringe.

This table cover is 42" square and made all in one piece. Make yours in the size needed, and divide the top into blocks if one piece is too much to handle. Make sure to purchase sufficient yardages for your particular table-cloth.

Finished size: 42" square

Materials

- Muslin for the foundation
- Scraps of cotton and other decorator fabrics for patches
- Wide eyelet lace and other cotton laces
- Fringe
- Cording
- Fabric for the backing
- Heavy brush fringe (cotton or rayon)
- Pearl cotton thread for the ties

(½" seam allowance)

TOOLBOX

✓ Topstitch Appliqué, page 8
✓ Fabrications, pages 139, 141

✓ Cordings, page 139
✓ Backing, page 138

Patch the Table Cover

1. Cut the muslin to the size needed, adding ½" seam allowance all around.

2. Patch the muslin in the Topstitch Appliqué method using the cordings and adding some fabricated patches. Refer to the photos for ideas for applying laces and trims.

3. Pin the heavy brush fringe along the edges right sides together, clipping at each corner to turn the corners, and butting the cut ends together.

Assemble the Table Cover

1. With right sides together, add the backing and pin.

2. Sew around, leaving an opening to turn.

3. Turn, press and slipstitch opening closed.

4. Use ties of pearl cotton to secure the patched top to the backing fabric, having the ties on the back.

Victoriana Fancy Box

Fancy crazy quilting, ribbonworked flowers, a tassel and other embellishments adorn a wooden box. The box lid is padded to give it dimension. Use the box to store keepsakes, cards, photos or supplies for your current needlework project. Assemble some pretty fabrics and trims and make a fancy box!

Finished size: 11" x 14"

Materials

- Unfinished wooden box, oval
- Acrylic paint in a complimentary color to the silk scraps for crazy patching
- Paintbrush
- Wallpaper (optional)
- Paper
- Pencil
- Scissors
- Organdy fabric for the foundation
- Lofty polyester batting
- White glue
- Silk scraps for crazy patching
- Trimmings such as a crocheted doily, mother-of-pearl buttons, wired ribbons for ribbonwork and a tassel
- Silk embroidery threads and silk ribbons for embroidery
- Trims of your choice for the lower edge of box lid

Prepare the Box

1. Set the lid of the box aside, and paint the box sides with the acrylic paint.

2. Paint or wallpaper the box and lid interior (or leave plain).

3. Make a paper pattern of the box lid by tracing around the outside of the lid. Cut out the pattern.

4. Using the pattern as a guide, cut the organdy fabric 1¼" larger than the pattern all around.

5. Cut two pieces of batting: make one the same size as the pattern. Make the other 1" smaller all around.

6. Center the smaller piece of batting on the box lid and glue it in place. Allow the glue to dry.

7. Drizzle glue lightly over the top of the glued batting and around it. Position the second piece of batting over the first. Place the lid upside down (on a surface that won't be damaged by glue) and weight it carefully with books until the glue dries.

TOOLBOX

✓ The Antique Method of Crazy Quilting, page 12

Embroidery Stitches, page 140

Patch and Embellish the Box Top

1. Patch the organdy foundation using the silk fabrics and the Antique Method.

2. Make and place on a woven ribbon patch (see instructions to the right).

3. Add the doily on top, then baste everything in place.

4. Embroider along the patch seams, working up to about 1" of the outer edge of the lid.

Woven Silk Ribbon Patches

Make your own patch fabrics by weaving silk or other ribbons. Using corrugated cardboard, pin lengths of ribbon next to each other. Cut additional lengths and weave them. You may want to put them into a dull needle or a bodkin to make this easier. When finished, unpin and transfer the weaving onto the foundation of your project. The weaving will be held intact when patches are laid onto its edges and basted.

5. Create a ribbonwork centerpiece (see instructions below).

6. Add a grouping of mother-of-pearl buttons.

Ribbon Flower Centerpiece

1. Begin with ribbons that are 1" to 1½" wide. Cut a piece of ribbon 18" to 20" long.

2. With a needle and thread, stitch along one edge, then pull up to gather. Coil the ribbon to form a rose, and sew through the bottom edge to hold it together.

3. Sew it to the foundation (adding prairie point leaves, if desired).

4. Make prairie point leaves by folding the ribbon into a triangular shape and gathering the wide end.

5. Sew on the prairie point along with a flower, concealing the raw edges under the flower.

6. For filler, make small gathered flowers out of ribbons that are ½" wide.

7. Tie a bow of 1" wide ribbon and pin it on while shaping it. Stitch in place.

8. Glue the organdy foundation to the box lid.

9. Working a section at a time, spread glue on the lower part of the box lid, then press the organdy in place. Hold until it is secured, then proceed to glue another section. It may be best to glue opposite edges in order to make it even. Allow the glue to dry, then if any edges protrude beyond the box lid, trim them even with the lid.

10. Apply trims to the lower part of the box lid. Be sure the trims cover this area entirely. Use plenty of glue, allowing it to dry between one trim and the next.

11. Seal the raw ends of the trims by coating them with glue.

The lower section of the box lid is trimmed with wide braided trim, metallic trim and cording.

Doll's Circle Skirt

A circle shape makes a very elegant skirt! Since most of the circle shape is on the bias, it drapes beautifully. It makes an elegant shape, going from wide at the hem up to a petite waist. And the skirt is all the more dramatic when crazy quilted with silk fabrics.

With these instructions, you can make a skirt for any size doll. For a special touch, include some hand-dyed silks.

This skirt makes use of silks fabric, such as jacquards, noil, Habotai, satin and some hand-dyed patches.

Materials

- Batiste or other fabric for the foundation
- Silk fabrics for the patches, including jacquards, noil, Habotai, silk satin and others
- Silk threads and silk ribbons for embroidery*
- Small mother-of-pearl buttons
- Hook and eye

*Used in this project: Kreinik's Silk Serica threads and YLI silk ribbons

Size the Pattern to Fit Your Doll

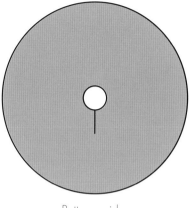

Pattern guide.

1. Measure the doll from waist to shoe to determine the length of the skirt. Add a couple of inches to allow for the cut-out center and hem.

2. Make a paper pattern for the circle.

3. Cut a small circle out of the center and hold the pattern up to the doll to see if it will fit her waist. Adjust the center to fit her waist, then check the length of the skirt. There should be an extra ½" or more at the bottom edge.

Patch and Embellish the Skirt

1. Cut the foundation fabric using the paper pattern.

2. Cut the smaller circle from the center and cut a slit in the skirt to make a placket (the slit will be placed in the back of the skirt).

3. Patch the foundation using the silk fabrics in the Antique Method of crazy patching.

4. Embroider along the patch edges, making one or two rows of stitches for each.

5. Embroider a small silk ribbon motif at the corners of some patches and sew a button onto others.

Finish the Skirt

1. To finish the back opening (placket) of the skirt, cut a strip of fabric about 1" wide by the length of the edges of the opening.

2. Sew the strip to the skirt right sides together, using a seam allowance of about ⅛".

3. Press the seam and press under the long raw edge of the strip of fabric.

4. Fold it to the back and slipstitch the folded edge over the seam. Fold the placket so it is inside the skirt.

5. To make a waistband, measure the waistline of the skirt and cut a strip of fabric this length plus 1".

6. Sew the strip of fabric to the skirt right sides together, and finish it the same as the placket, making sure to instead fold in and slipstitch the ends. The waistband finishes to the outside of the skirt.

7. Add a hook and eye closure.

Making Doll Clothes

It's been many years since I sat on my mother's sewing room floor and cut scraps of fabric and sewed them into clothes for my dolls. The experience has stayed with me all these years; I still make doll clothes in much the same way. There's been some improvement; the doll clothes I make now not only fit the dolls better, but they are considerably more fancy. I've tried using patterns and making my own patterns, but I still think the best method is to fit the fabrics right on the doll. If you are using scraps anyway, what difference does it make if you don't cut something right the first time? Just do it over again!

It can help to have a basic understanding of garment sewing, especially in cutting things like blouses, in which armholes and sleeve tops are cut a certain way. But don't let this deter you. If you feel like a dressing a doll, go ahead and give it a try. The first things I ever sewed were doll clothes!

TOOLBOX

✓ The Antique Method of Crazy Quilting, page 12 ✓ Circle Pattern, page 139 ✓ Embroidery Stitches, page 140

Chapter 4

Country Capers!

Country Heart

To make a similar heart, work feather stitch embroidery on Confetti Piecing. Edge the heart with self-made cording. Sew on a cluster of buttons and add seed beads along the embroidery stitches. Sew on some beaded fringe. Make a tassel out of several colors of pearl cotton thread, then tie on some brass charms.

TOOLBOX

✓ Confetti Piecing, page 10
✓ Feather Stitch, page 140
✓ Self-Made Cordings, page 139
✓ Beaded Fringe, page 138

✓ A Basic Tassel, page 142
✓ Heart Pattern, page 15
✓ Backing, page 138

Rolling Hills Wallhanging

Materials

- Large sheets of paper
- Pencil
- Scissors
- ¼ yd. lengths of 20 different 100 percent cotton quilting fabrics in reds, greens, golds and peaches in light to dark shades
- 6 to 8 blue cotton quilting fabrics in shades from pale to dark for the sky
- 1¾ yd. of 100 percent cotton muslin for the foundations
- ¼" wide medium green ribbon to create farmlands and to decorate the rolling hills
- ¼" wide light green ribbon to create farmlands and to decorate the rolling hills
- Narrow flowery trims to decorate the rolling hills
- Upholstery trims at least ½" wide to edge the rolling hills
- Venices, cotton laces in natural and white to edge the rolling hills
- Rayon cordings in burgundy, dark green and rose to edge the rolling hills
- Stabilizer
- 1¾ yd. backing fabric such as a plain cotton quilting fabric
- Sewing threads to match the ribbons and trims
- White quilting thread
- Pearl cotton, size 8, in a color to blend with the hills

Cutting Instructions

From the various quilting fabrics for the binding:

- Cut strips 2⅛" x the length or width of the fabric
- Recut each strip into 3" lengths.

From the foundation fabric:

- Cut one piece 34" x 35"
- Cut two pieces 10" x 35"

From the backing fabric:

- Cut one piece 34" x 35"
- Cut two pieces 10" x 35"

For the love of beautiful rolling hills, farmlands and fields stretching far into the distance and fading into a pale sky ... This wallhanging is Confetti-Pieced and assembled in the Topstitch Appliqué method. Make this project the size and shape of your choice.

TOOLBOX

✓ Confetti Piecing, page 10
✓ Rod Pocket, page 142
✓ Tie the Quilt, page 143
✓ Bias Binding, page 138

Prepare the Patterns

1. Cut the paper to one 34" x 35" piece to make a center panel and two 10" x 35" pieces to make the two side panels.

2. Sketch rolling hills onto each paper panel, making the hills smaller as they fade into the distance (see the diagram). Cut out each hill as it is needed (see instructions below).

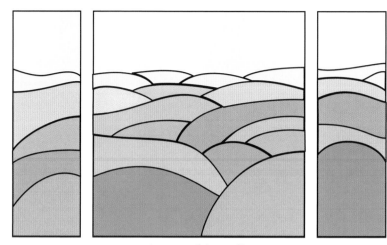

Layout diagram of the wallhanging.

Patch the Hills and Sky

1. Work Confetti Piecing to make the hills. Vary the mixes of fabrics as you make the sections. Make some in deep colors for the foreground hills, some in the lightest shades for the farthest ones and mix dark and light shades for the hills in the middle. As you make the Confetti sections, cut the hills out of them. Butt them together. The trims will cover all of the raw edges later.

2. Cut one Confetti piece for each of the hill pattern pieces. As you do, pin the hills in their places on the three foundations.

3. Work Confetti Piecing using the sky blue fabrics to make one sky section for each of the panels.

4. Lay the sky pieces in place on the foundations. Pin. (They can underlap the farthest rolling hills.)

5. Choose some of the hills to create farmland. One at at time, unpin and make furrows by sewing on the medium green ribbon for the nearer hills and the light green ribbon for the farther hills. Use a zigzag machine stitch that covers the ribbon, having the needle plunk down on both sides of it, with stabilizer underneath. Make the furrows curved as shown, placing the ribbons about ¼" to ½" apart.

6. Apply narrow flowery trims in meandering lines on a few of the hills.

7. Baste the hills and sky in place.

Embellish the Hills

1. One hill at a time, and using stabilizer if needed, machine stitch trims to the upper edge of each hill. Vary the trims so they are different for each hill.

Note: Begin with the most underlapped hill, farthest away. If you don't begin with the farthest hill, you will be opening up seams later on—trims applied later cover the raw edges of those applied earlier.

2. Sew on a piece of lace or Venice, facing it either downward or upward. Then sew on ½" or wider trim. Use this trim to cover the raw edge of the lace and one half of the raw edge of the Confetti Piecing. Sew along both edges of the trim.

3. Hand sew a piece of cording using the darker colors for the foreground hills and the rose for the farthest hills. This provides a distinct outline for each hill.

Assemble the Wallhanging

1. Lay the backing fabric on the back of the panels, matching the sizes, and baste all around. Pin or baste throughout the panels.

2. Quilt the three sky sections, stitching in the ditch, using white quilting thread.

3. Using pearl cotton, tie the layers throughout the hill areas, making the ties on the back.

4. To make the binding, use ¼" seam allowance to sew the 2⅛" x 3" strips together to make sides, top and bottom bindings for each panel. Use the darker colors for the lower parts of each panel and the lighter colors for the upper parts. The top and bottom borders will be the same length as the widths of the panels. Make the side bindings 1" longer than the length of the panels.

5. Using ½" seam allowance, sew the top and bottom bindings to each panel. Press to the back, fold in the raw edge and slipstitch.

6. Using ½" seam allowance, sew the side bindings to each panel, clean finishing the upper and lower edges while slipstitching.

7. Make and sew a rod pocket to the back of each panel.

Note: Make sure to sew the rod pockets at equal distances from the top of each panel so they hang evenly.

Americana Bellpull

Materials

- ¼ yd. muslin for the foundation
- ¼ yd. fabric for the backing
- ¼ yd. lengths of 8 different greens of cotton quilting fabric for Confetti Piecing
- Scraps of faded red, faded blue and white cotton quilting fabrics for the flag ends
- Scraps of dark green and dark red quilting fabrics for the checkerboard
- Trims
- Laces
- Ribbons
- 14" narrow gold welting
- 1⅛" wide gold strips for the binding
- Pearl cotton for the ties and embroidery in dark red, blue and gold

Cutting Instructions

From the white scraps:
- Cut two 3½" squares for the flag
- Cut two strips each 1½" x 3½" for the flag

From the red scraps:
- Cut four strips each 1½" x 3½" for the flag
- Cut one strip 1½" x the length of the scrap for the checkerboard. Recut crosswise into 1½" sections.

From the dark green scraps:
- Cut one strip 1½" x the length of the scrap for the checkerboard. Recut crosswise into 1½" sections.

From the muslin:
- Cut one 6½" x 12½" foundation piece.

From the backing fabric:
- Cut one 6½" x 24½" backing piece.

(¼" seam allowance)

Checkerboard quilting, pieced and appliquéd flags and Confetti-Pieced rolling hills give this bellpull a feel of "Americana."

TOOLBOX

✓ French Knot, page 140
✓ Rod Pocket, page 142
✓ Checkerboarding, page 139

✓ Bias Strips and Bias Bindings, pages 138-139
✓ Appliqué, page 138

✓ Welting, page 143
✓ Tie the Quilt, page 143

Make the Flags

Layout diagram of the bellpull.

1. Trace the star pattern and cut it out.

2. Use the pattern to appliqué a star onto each of the 3½" white squares.

3. Sew the red and white strips to make two flags (see the photo for placement).

4. Sew on the star sections to the striped sections.

5. To make the checkerboard, sew the red and dark green 1½" sections together to make checkerboards, alternating squares, as shown in the photo.

6. Sew welting to one long edge of each checkerboard.

7. Sew the flags to the same edge.

Patch the Hills

1. Make the hills following instructions in the Patching and Embellishing sections of the Rolling Hills Wallhanging (see page 84). You can make a pattern for the hills or just fit them into place on the muslin foundation.

Assemble the Bellpull

1. Sew a checkerboard and flag piece to each end.

2. Embroider the flag sections as desired.

3. Place the backing fabric on the back of the piece and pin.

4. Sew strips of binding to the side edges.

5. Fold the binding to the back, press under and slipstitch.

6. Bind the top and bottom edges, finishing the ends of the binding neatly.

7. If desired, embroider French knots along the inner edges of the binding.

8. Place gold ties in the centers of the dark green blocks of the checkerboards.

9. Add a rod pocket or loops to the back for hanging.

Star

Chicken on a Stick

Make a crazy quilted chicken for a centerpiece or to decorate a sideboard. Because it is made with a dowel, this is a soft sculpture, not a child's toy.

Materials

- Tracing paper
- Pencil
- Scissors
- ¼ yd. lengths of 100 percent cotton quilting fabrics in 8 different colors in deep rusty reds and golds
- Scraps of red and gold fabric
- ⅓ yd. of 100 percent cotton muslin fabric
- Dollmaker's needle (this is a long hand sewing needle)
- Stuffing
- Dowel
- Wooden base
- Glue

(¼" seam allowance)

Patch the Chicken Body

1. Trace the pattern pieces on pages 92-93 and cut them out.

2. Use the quilting fabrics to Confetti-Piece two pieces each the size of the chicken body pattern plus the two gusset pieces.

3. Cut out the pieces.

4. Cut the same from the muslin.

Assemble the Chicken

1. Cut the remaining pattern pieces using red fabric for the comb and wattle, gold for the beak and the golds and reds of your choice for the feathers. Make 12 large feathers and eight small feathers.

2. Stitching right at the edges, sew the muslin pieces to the backs of the Confetti pieces.

3. Sew a beak to each chicken body half.

> **TOOLBOX**
> ✓ Confetti Piecing, page 10

4. Fold and press the wider short end of each gusset piece.

Leave opening for stuffing

5. With right sides together, sew one long edge of each gusset piece to one of the chicken halves. Have the folded ends of the gusset meet at the center with no gap.

6. With right sides together, sew the remaining long edges of the gusset to the other chicken half. Leave a 2" section of the seam unsewn for stuffing later.

7. Beginning at one end of the gusset, sew the chicken halves right sides together. End the stitching at the other end of the gusset.

8. Trim, turn and press. Slipstitch the opening closed.

Add the Dowel

1. Stuff the chicken firmly while inserting the dowel into the opening of the gusset. Place the dowel all the way in so it lightly touches the chicken's back.

2. When finished stuffing the chicken, push the glue bottle in beside the dowel and squeeze out enough glue so the dowel will be secured to some of the stuffing to prevent slippage. Allow the glue to dry.

3. Hand stitch around the dowel to close the opening in the gusset.

Finish the Chicken

1. Leaving an opening to turn, sew the comb and wattle pieces right sides together.

2. Trim, turn and press. Insert a very small amount of stuffing and slipstitch the openings closed.

3. Hand stitch the comb and wattle invisibly to the chicken, matching seams.

4. With right sides together, sew the seams of the feathers, leaving an opening to turn.

5. Trim, turn and press. Slipstitch the openings closed.

6. Arrange three large feathers and one small feather on each side of the chicken and pin. Thread the doll-maker's needle with a long, doubled length of thread. Knot it and sew through the chicken from one side to the other, making any knots appear under the feathers, and making tiny fastening stitches on the surfaces of the feathers.

7. Arrange the remaining feathers along the tail, half of the feathers on each side, and pin. Sew in place using the dollmaker's needle as before.

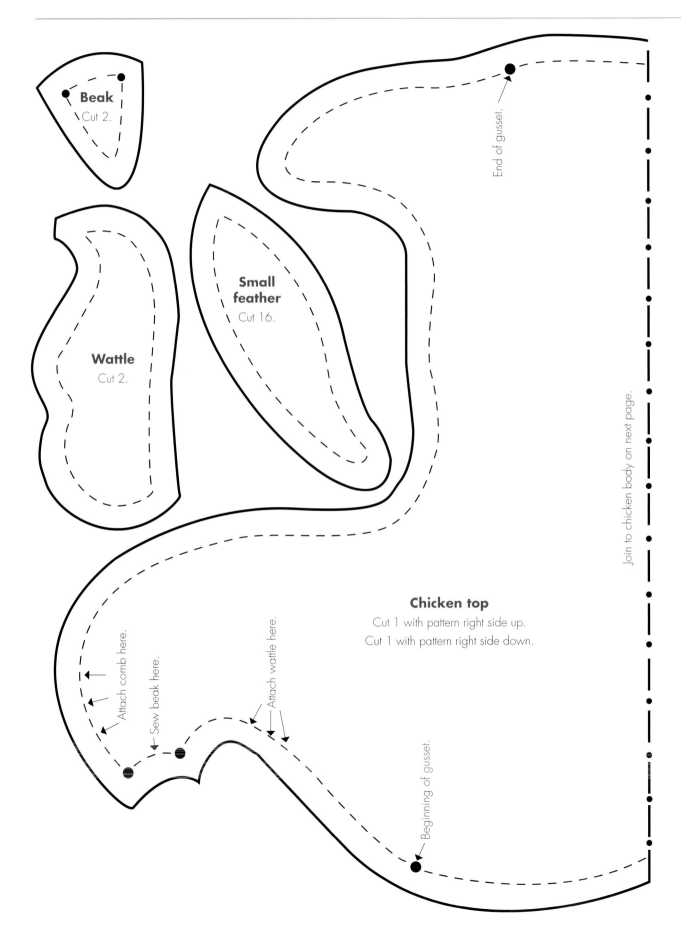

Beak
Cut 2.

Wattle
Cut 2.

Small feather
Cut 16.

Chicken top
Cut 1 with pattern right side up.
Cut 1 with pattern right side down.

End of gusset.

Join to chicken body on next page.

Attach comb here.

Sew beak here.

Attach wattle here.

Beginning of gusset.

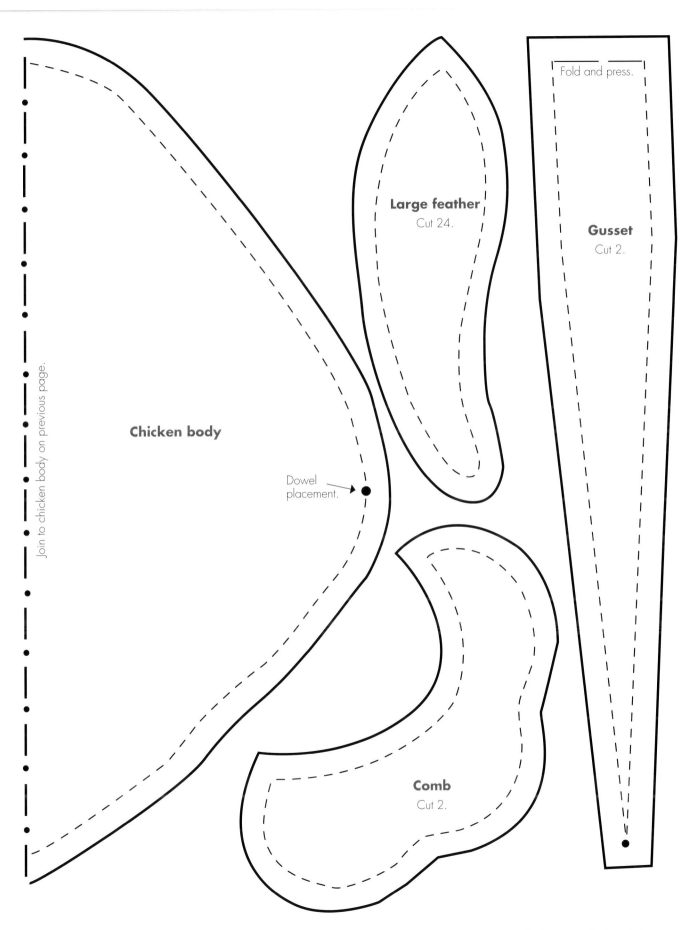

Join to chicken body on previous page.

Chicken body

Dowel placement.

Large feather
Cut 24.

Gusset
Cut 2.

Fold and press.

Comb
Cut 2.

Three-Piece Dining Set

Bow-Tie Table Center

The dining set includes a table center ringed with fabric bows, a chair topper and a coiled cushion.

Yellow and white are room brighteners, and this table center with its white fabric bows will give a feeling of springtime all year round.

Materials

- Large sheet of paper
- Pencil
- Ruler
- Tracing paper
- Scissors
- ¼ yd. each of 8 or more 100 percent cotton quilting fabrics in yellows and whites
- ⅔ yd. white cotton fabric for the backing and ties
- 20" square of batting
- White quilting thread
- Safety pin or tube turner

(¼" seam allowance)

Patch the Circle

1. Use the large piece of paper, pencil and ruler to make a 20" circle.

2. Using the cotton quilting fabrics, work Confetti Piecing to make one piece the same size as the paper circle pattern.

3. Use the paper pattern to cut a piece of batting the same size.

4. Fold the paper pattern in half and cut two half circles of backing fabric, adding ¼" seam allowance along the straight edge.

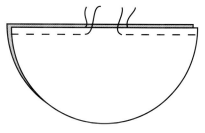

5. Sew the center seam of the backing, leaving about 5" at the center unsewn. Set aside.

TOOLBOX

✔ Confetti Piecing, page 10   ✔ Circle Pattern, page 139   ✔ Machine Quilting, page 141

Make the Bows

1. Trace and cut out the bow pattern.

2. Use the pattern to cut pieces for 12 bows out of the white fabric (24 pieces in all).

3. Place two bow pieces right sides together and sew, leaving an opening at the center.

4. Trim, turn and press. You do not need to sew the openings closed—just press the seam allowance inward.

5. Out of the white fabric, cut two pieces each 1½" x 36".

6. Place the two pieces right sides together and sew along the long edges. Trim the seam.

7. Using a safety pin or tube turner, turn right-side out and press. Cut the piece into 3" lengths for ties.

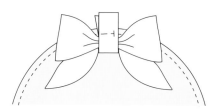

8. To make the bows, take one bow and fold along the fold lines indicated on the pattern. Fold one of the 3" lengths around the center of the tie. Hold onto the tops of the tie and push the bow down toward the fold. Hold it in place and insert a pin through the tie to hold the bow in place.

9. Arrange the bows evenly around the Confetti circle and pin each in place along the seam allowance.

10. Hand or machine baste each tie in place. Place a pin in each bow to hold it away from the seamline so that only the centers will be sewn into the seam.

Finish the Table Center

1. Place the batting behind the Confetti piece. Place the backing on top, right sides together. Pin, then sew around.

2. Turn the piece through the opening in the backing. Press. Slipstitch the opening closed.

3. Pin or baste throughout the table center.

4. Machine quilt in rows 1" apart.

5. Arrange the bows neatly and slipstitch them in place, leaving the tail ends free.

Bow

Foldline

Place on fold of fabric.

Chair Topper with Bows

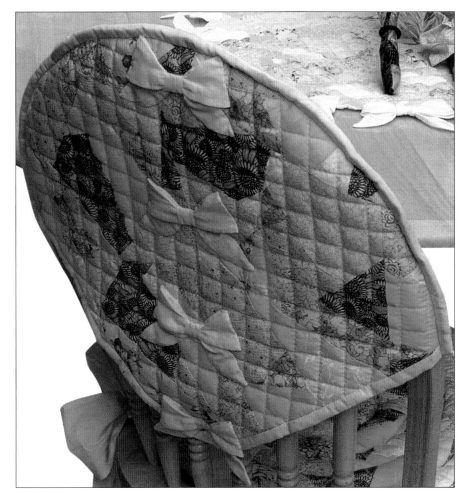

Materials

- Newspaper or large piece of paper
- Pencil
- Scissors
- ¼ yd. lengths of 6 to 8 different 100 percent cotton quilting fabrics in yellows and white, sufficient for several toppers
- Backing fabric: pattern x 2
- Batting: pattern x 2
- White quilting thread
- ¼ yd. white cotton fabric for the ties and binding
- Snap fastener or Velcro

(½" seam allowance)

Dress your chairs in bow-tied toppers! These are designed for chairs with rounded backs, but with a little imagination, toppers can be made for most other types of chairs. Make a newspaper pattern by draping the paper, then decide how to shape the piece.

The fabric amounts needed depend on the size of the chair topper. You may wish to make the paper pattern first, then purchase appropriate amounts according to the pattern. Amounts given are for one topper. Purchase sufficient yardage and materials for the number of chairs you have.

TOOLBOX

✓ Confetti Piecing, page 10

✓ Bias Strips and Bias Bindings, pages 139, 141

✓ Machine Quilting, page 141

✓ Bow Pattern, page 95

Make a Pattern to Fit Your Chair

1. Make a paper pattern using the newspaper or large piece of paper. Lay the chair down and follow the lines of the chair back with the pencil. Shape the bottom into a "V." Repeat for a second pattern.

2. Tape the two patterns together and place it onto the chair back to make sure the topper will fit correctly. If not, make changes until the topper fits.

3. Make a final pattern, adding about ⅛" for ease and ½" all around for the seam allowance (for a total of about ⅞" extra all around).

Place the chair back on a pillow to make it easier to trace its outline.

Patch the Chair Topper

1. Make two Confetti pieces using the cotton quilting fabrics in yellows and white, cutting each the same as the pattern.

2. Cut two backings and two battings using the pattern.

3. Make two pieces, each consisting of: the backing fabric right side down, batting and Confetti piece right side up. Pin, baste and quilt.

4. Cut bias for the binding 2⅛" wide.

5. Bind the lower edges of each piece.

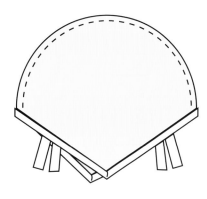

Make and Attach the Ties

1. Using the white cotton fabric, cut four pieces each 2" wide by 15" long for the ties.

2. Place two together and sew along two sides and one end. Turn and press. Repeat for a second tie.

3. Baste the raw ends of the ties to the top of the chair topper backing (so they will be on the inside of the finished topper).

4. With wrong sides together, sew the topper front and back sections together (the seam will be on outside).

5. Bind the upper edge, finishing the ends neatly.

Make and Attach the Bows

1. Trace the bow pattern and cut it out. Cut four bows from the white fabric.

2. Fold each of the four bows along the fold lines indicated on the pattern given on page 95.

3. For the centers, cut four strips 1¼" x 2".

4. Fold the strips lengthwise and sew them into a tube using ¼" seam allowance. Turn and press.

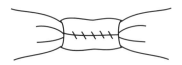

5. Fold ¼" in from one end.

6. Beginning at the open end, fold the center around the bow, overlapping the ends, and stitch. The bow will be slightly scrunched.

7. Arrange the bows along the center back of the chair topper (refer to the photo on page 96 for placement) and slipstitch in place, stitching through the back parts of the bow.

8. To finish the topper, sew a snap or a small piece of Velcro inside the bottom edge.

Coiled Confetti Chair Cushion

Rolled quilt batting covered in Confetti Piecing makes a plump and cozy chair cushion. Make your cushions the size needed for your chair seats. Amounts given are for one cushion. Purchase sufficient yardage and materials for the number of chairs you have.

Materials

- ¼ yd. lengths of 6 to 8 different 100 percent cotton quilting fabrics in yellows and white, sufficient for several cushions
- 100 percent cotton sewing thread
- 1½ yd. high-loft polyester batting (57" wide)
- Hand sewing needle
- ½ yd. smooth white cotton fabric for the ties

(½" seam allowance for assembly)

Roll the Batting to Make the Coil

1. To determine the amount of batting needed, lay the batting out flat. Take one edge of it and begin rolling, but not tightly or loosely.

2. Measure to find the circumference, and when it is 5", mark and then unroll the batting and measure to find the amount of batting required to make a 5" roll. This could be around 10" or so, depending on your batting.

3. Cut enough batting the same amount to total about 5 yards (or the amount needed to fit your chair).

4. Take one piece of batting and, beginning at the center, roll it into one long coil and pin.

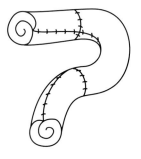

5. Loosely hand stitch just enough to hold the roll. Repeat for remaining batting.

6. Butt the ends of the rolls up next to each other to make one long piece. Join them by hand stitching.

7. Coil it to see if it fits your chair. Adjust the length as needed. Set aside.

TOOLBOX

✓ Confetti Piecing, page 10   ✓ Slipstitching, page 142

Patch the Fabric for the Coil

1. Using the quilting fabrics, work Confetti Piecing to make a long piece that is 6½" wide by 5 yards long, plus a couple of inches to finish the ends.

2. Fold in one long edge ½" and press. Also press under the seam allowance at one end.

3. Lay the rolled batting onto the wrong side of the Confetti band, having one end about 1" in from the folded end of the banding. Roll the banding around the tube, pin and slipstitch.

4. Finish the beginning end. Run a gathering thread along the fold, pull tight to gather and fasten off. Slipstitch along the length of the banding.

Coil the Cushion

1. To prepare for coiling, thread a needle with doubled thread or use a heavy type of thread. Fasten on at the gathered end. Make short stitches along the slipstitched seam, stopping at intervals to pull up and gather. Pull the gathering thread just until the roll coils into place. Continue to the end. This step allows the piece to coil smoothly.

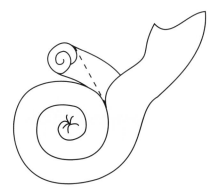

2. To finish the other (outer) end, first cut the rolled batting, as shown in the diagram above. Fold the banding over the cut end and stitch neatly.

3. Using a heavy or doubled thread, begin again at the gathered (inner) end, and proceed to stitch the coils together. Keep the seam running along the center where it will be concealed. When finished, you may want to flip the cushion over and work an additional line of stitching. This will make the cushion sturdier.

Make and Attach the Ties

1. To make a pair of ties for the cushion, cut four strips of white fabric each 43" long by 3¾" wide.

2. Sew two of the strips together and cut the ends in the shape shown in the diagram below. Repeat for the other two pieces. Sew around, leaving an opening to turn.

3. Turn, press and slipstitch the opening closed.

4. Place the cushion on the chair to determine the placements of the ties. Find the center of each tie and tack them to the cushion, gathering the tie as you do so.

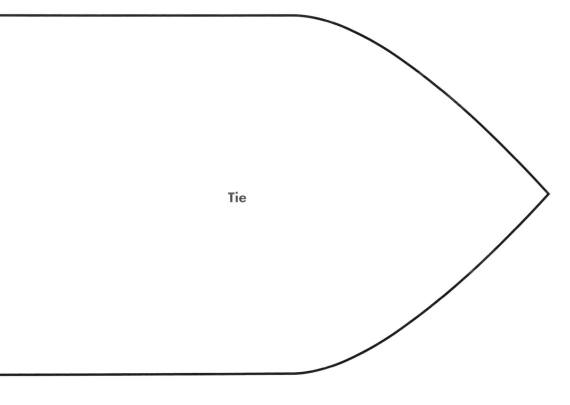

Tie

Raggy Pillow

This is a wash, toss and wear pillow. Washing it makes it better by fluffing up the exposed raw edges of the seams and fabric fringes. Make the pillow any size desired, from a small throw pillow to a large floor pillow.

Materials

- 8 different 100 percent cotton printed fabrics for Confetti Piecing
- 100 percent cotton muslin fabric, white
- 1 to 2 yd. 100 percent cotton fabric for bullion fringe, white
- Fabric for the backing
- Pillow insert the size of your pillow

(½" seam allowance)

Layer and Patch the Fabrics

1. Decide on the size of your pillow adding 1" in each direction for seam allowances.

2. Back each piece of cotton printed fabric with two layers of the cotton muslin fabric, creating three layers. Handle the three layers as if they were one.

3. Work Confetti Piecing according to instructions, **except** make the seams on the right side. Each seam sewn will create an exposed seam allowance that is six layers thick.

Make and Attach the Bullion Fringe

1. To make the bullion fringe, begin with a yard of cotton fabric and cut rounded edges.

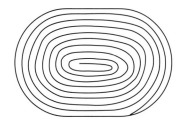

2. Then begin cutting from the outside, working your way to the middle. Cut a continuous strip about ⅞" wide.

3. Wind the strip into a ball.

4. Cut a 15" length from the strip. Follow instructions for making cording, twisting the strip into a fringe.

5. Pin the fringe to the pillow top, as shown in the diagram above. Continue to make fringes and pin them on.

6. After a section is worked, machine baste the fringe ends and remove the pins. Continue around the pillow top until it is completely fringed.

Finish the Pillow

1. Make a pillow back using the overlap method.

2. Machine wash and dry the pillow cover. Trim away any excessive ravels.

3. Insert the pillow form into the pillow cover.

TOOLBOX

✓ Confetti Piecing, page 10   ✓ Cordings, page 139   ✓ Overlapped Pillow Backing, page 9

Crazy Patches Curtain

Materials

- Plain, unlined curtain
- ¼ yd. lengths of 8 different 100 percent cotton printed fabrics
- Quilting thread*

*Used in this project: YLI quilting thread

Patch the Fabric for the Squares

1. Decide on the size of the squares you want for the curtain.

2. Work Confetti Piecing large enough for your desired number of squares.

3. Cut the number needed from the Confetti piece, adding ¼" seam allowances.

Attach the Squares to the Curtain

1. Press the seam allowances to the back and slipstitch the squares in place on the curtain.

2. Machine sew lines of quilting from the top to the bottom of the curtain, making a swirl pattern on each Confetti square.

3. For added decoration, randomly sew on small squares of cotton fabric, and ravel the edges.

Add a touch of crazy quilting to an existing plain curtain. When the light shines through the curtain, the patches will give it a stained glass effect.

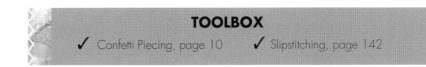

TOOLBOX

✓ Confetti Piecing, page 10   ✓ Slipstitching, page 142

Fold-Back Curtain Panel

Only the folded-back portion of this curtain panel is crazy quilted. Elegant in its cottage-style simplicity, it is a flat curtain without gathering or ruffles. Installation hardware for a panel curtain can be as creative a concept as you can devise. Use small drawer knobs, fancy hooks, wooden pegs, old square nails or anything else you can think of (or make the curtain with a rod pocket and place it on a curtain rod).

TOOLBOX

✓ Confetti Piecing, page 10

Materials

- 100 percent cotton fabric for the plain part of the panel
- 100 percent cotton fabric for lining (can be the same fabric as above)
- ¼ yd. lengths of 6 to 8 different 100 percent cotton quilting fabrics
- 1 brass or bone ring
- Hardware to fasten the curtain to the window (see above)

(¼" seam allowance unless otherwise noted)

Determine the Size of the Curtain Panel

1. Measure the window to determine the finished size of the panel. You can make one panel for a small window or two for a larger window. Add ½" seam allowance to the width and 2½" to the length.

2. Use these dimensions to cut out the lining part of the panel.

3. Tape the lining to the window where it will be placed (the extra 2¼" in length will be at the top for the header).

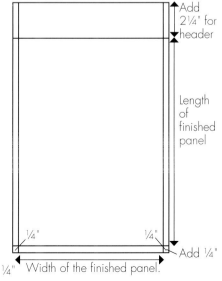

Add 2¼" for header

Length of finished panel

¼"   ¼"

Add ¼"

¼" Width of the finished panel.

Diagram of the seam allowances.

Patch the Fabric for the Corner

1. Fold back the bottom corner and pin it to the curtain to keep the fold. Take down the lining and press along the fold.

2. Work Confetti Piecing the same size as the folded corner of the panel, adding ¼" for the seam allowance along the fold.

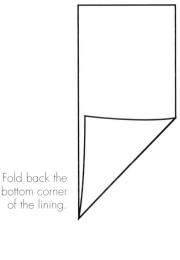

Fold back the bottom corner of the lining.

Assemble the Curtain Panel

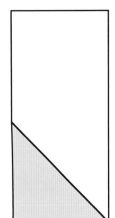

1. With right sides together, pin the seam placement of the Confetti piece to the fold on the right side (the side that faces the window) of the lining.

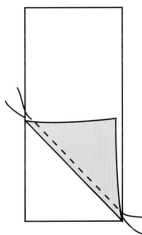

2. Sew along the fold line. Trim away the excess lining under the Confetti piece.

3. Cut the plain fabric part of the panel.

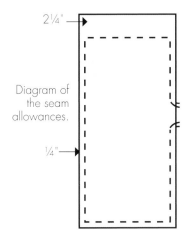

2¼"

¼"

Diagram of the seam allowances.

4. Sew the plain panel to the lining right sides together, using ¼" seam allowance along the sides and bottom of the panel and a 2¼" seam allowance at the top. Leave an opening to turn.

5. Turn, press and slipstitch the opening closed.

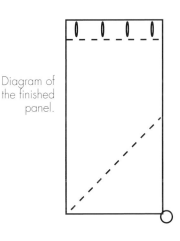

Diagram of the finished panel.

6. Sew 2" from the top of the curtain to make the header. Depending on the width of the panel, make three to four buttonholes in the header, making them 1" long and spaced evenly. (I used four in a curtain that is 21" wide).

7. Sew the bone ring to the corner that will be folded back.

The Collage Method of Crazy Quilting

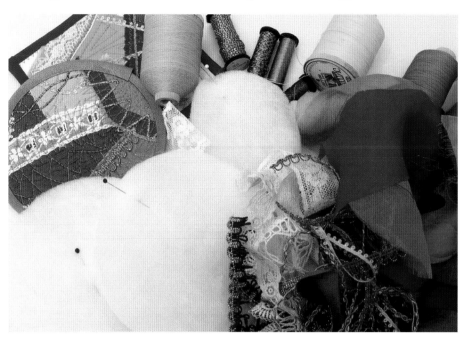

This method creates a flat surface making it ideal for such things as coasters. It is an artful, "free" method of laying and attaching patches with no concern to turning under the edges. Machine sewing covers all trims, uniting the pieces by causing colors to blend.

1. Begin with any sturdy foundation fabric. Use what is appropriate for your project. Optional: You can add a piece of batting on top of the foundation.

2. Lay the fabrics onto the foundation, arranging them as desired. They should overlap onto each other and leave no foundation showing. If necessary, machine sew them to hold them in place.

3. Add some trims on top of the fabrics.

4. Begin sewing anywhere on the piece. I like to use quilting thread in a color that adds to the piece. Do plenty of stitching so all fabrics and trims are held in place. The raw edges of the patches will ravel, adding to the effect.

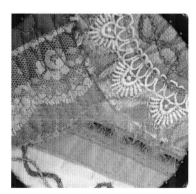

Materials

- Paper
- Pencil
- Scissors
- Cotton organdy fabric for the foundation
- Small fabric scraps, laces, trims and cordings
- Batting
- Fabric for the backing
- Fabric for the bias binding
- Colored quilting thread*
- Seed beads (optional)
- Beading needle (optional)
- Beading thread (optional)

*Used in this project: YLI colored quilting thread

Collage Coasters

The collage method is great for making coasters because it leaves a flat surface. Add snazzy detail to your coasters with a colorful binding and beads.

TOOLBOX

✓ The Collage Method of Crazy Quilting, page 104

✓ Bias Strips and Bias Binding, pages 138-139

✓ Beading, page 138

Patch the Coaster Top

1. Make paper patterns for the size and shape of the coaster desired. The circular coasters shown here are 5" in diameter.

2. Cut your desired shape out of organdy fabric and batting.

3. Follow instructions for the Collage Method to patch and add trims to the organdy fabric and batting.

Assemble the Coaster

1. Using the pattern, cut the backing fabric.

2. Place one backing on each of the collage pieces. Pin or baste.

3. Make and sew bias binding around each coaster.

4. If desired, sew on seed beads to make decorative edgings.

Charmed Napkin Ring

Charms are great fun to add to napkin rings! They truly make a napkin ring delightful. Your guests will pick it up, shake it to make it jingle, then carefully examine each charm. Instructions are for one napkin ring. Repeat to make the number needed for your table settings.

Materials

- 2¾" x 9" piece of buckram or any sturdy foundation material
- 2¾" x 9" batting
- 2¾" x 9" piece of fabric for the backing
- Small fabric scraps, laces, trims and cordings
- Colored quilting thread*
- Fabric for the bias binding
- Several buttons
- Charms

Used in this project: YLI quilting thread

Patch the Napkin Ring Top

1. Using the buckram as the foundation, place the batting on top.

2. Place the fabric scraps, laces, trim and cordings on the batting and proceed with the Collage Method.

Assemble the Napkin Ring

1. Place the backing fabric on the back of the buckram and pin or baste.

2. Cut bias strips 1⅛" wide to make the binding.

3. Sew the binding to the edges of the napkin ring.

4. Roll the piece into a circle, overlapping the ends 1½".

5. Sew on a cluster of buttons to fasten.

6. Sew on the charms, spacing them evenly along each side edge.

TOOLBOX

✓ The Collage Method of Crazy Quilting, page 104   ✓ Bias Strips and Bias Binding, pages 138-139

Missy RagMuffin

It's such a neat thing to share space with a rag doll! Sit her on a chair, bookshelf or wherever she fits in your home.

Dolls gain character as you work on them. Face, hair, clothes and jewelry all add to her personality. You may find yourself searching for a name as you work on her. And, in the end, something comical in her expression will make you giggle.

Missy's body is made of Confetti Piecing. Because of this, she doesn't really need clothes. Make a little pair of shorts, as Missy has, or a skirt. Put some buttons on her front and some ribbon bows on her "shoe tops."

This doll can be made so she is "kid-friendly." For small children, do not use things like buttons or necklaces that can be pulled off. Sew hair on securely. She will then be a piece of your décor that can be played with.

Materials

- ¼ yd. lengths of 6 to 8 different 100 percent cotton quilting fabrics
- ¼ yd. muslin fabric
- Stuffing
- Materials of your choice for finishing the doll including embroidery threads for the features, yarn or thread for hair, etc.

(¼" seam allowance)

TOOLBOX
✓ Confetti Piecing, page 10

Patch the Pattern Pieces

1. Cut out the pattern pieces on pages 108 and 109.

2. Work Confetti Piecing to make enough for each pattern piece, then cut them out.

Assemble the Doll

1. Using the patterns, cut the muslin.

2. Place a muslin piece on the back of each Confetti piece and handle the two as one.

3. Place two arm pieces right sides together and sew around, leaving the shoulder end open. Repeat for the second arm and both legs.

4. Turn the limbs right-side out and stuff. To make a floppy doll, keep the stuffing loose toward the tops of the limbs.

5. Pin the arms to the body front piece so the thumbs will be facing upward after sewing.

6. Bring together the two seams at the top of one leg. This will make the toes face upward. Pin the leg to the body front. Repeat for the other leg.

7. Place the body back and front pieces right sides together and sew, leaving an opening in one of the sides. As you sew around, let the arms and legs come through this opening rather than be stuffed inside the body. Clip seams as needed, especially in the neck area.

8. Turn right-side out, stuff the body firmly and slipstitch the opening closed.

Add Details

1. Choose embroidery colors that will show up on her face and embroider mouth, cheeks and nose.

2. Sew on buttons for eyes and embroider the eyelashes.

3. Using a large needle, sew on some yarn for hair, and style as desired.

4. Sew on buttons for her "shirt front."

5. Make and sew on ribbon bows for her "shoe tops."

Sew "hair" to seamline

Missy RagMuffin Body

¼" seam allowances are included.

Cut 2 of Confetti.
Cut 2 of muslin.

Leave opening to turn.

Place on fold of fabric.

Enlarge 125%

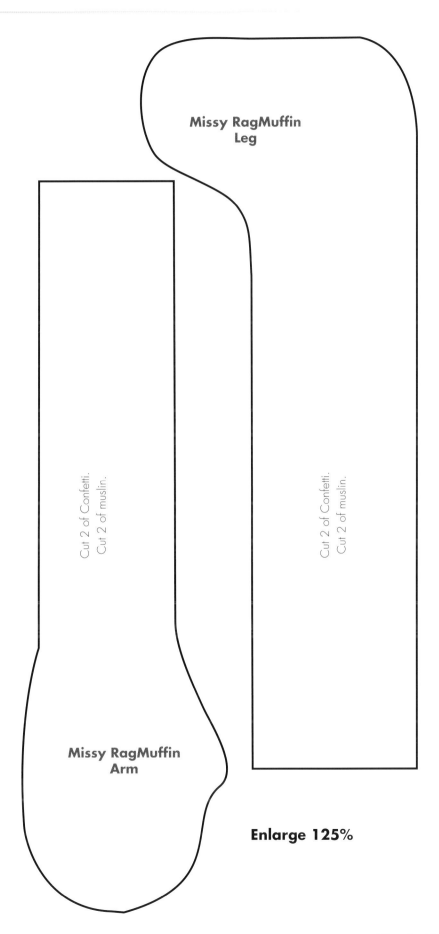

**Missy RagMuffin
Leg**

**Missy RagMuffin
Arm**

Cut 2 of Confetti.
Cut 2 of muslin.

Cut 2 of Confetti.
Cut 2 of muslin.

Enlarge 125%

Chapter 5

Waxing Whimsical!

Whimsy Heart

Use Confetti Piecing to make this heart. Quilt it in a colorful thread, then add some tufts and sew on a bright button. Edge the heart with self-made cording and make a tassel using rayon embroidery floss and a glitzy novelty yarn. Make smaller tassels and sew them onto the wrappings of the larger one.

TOOLBOX

✔ Confetti Piecing, page 10
✔ Cording, page 139
✔ A Basic Tassel, page 142
✔ Heart Pattern, page 15

✔ Backing, page 138
✔ Tufts, page 112
✔ Machine Quilting, page 141

Shower Curtain Topper

Here is a way to add a touch of crazy quilting to the shower décor without having to patch an entire shower curtain. Hang this topper with a vinyl or fabric shower curtain, using the same hooks.

This topper consists of ten panels which will fit a standard size bathtub. If your shower is a different width than a standard bathtub, measure it, then make the correct number of panels to fit.

Materials

- ¼ yd. lengths of 100 percent cotton quilting fabrics in 8 different colors
- 1 yd. muslin
- 1 yd. 100 percent cotton fabric for the backing
- Quilting thread in 2 colors*
- Pearl cotton thread, size 8
- 17 yd. each of 3 different purchased cordings or trims such as rattail or rayon cording (per panel)
- 3 yd. eyelet lace (2½" wide)

*Used in this project: YLI Quilting Thread

(¼" seam allowance)

Braided Trim

The trim used on the following three projects consists of two purchased cordings and rattail, which are braided together.
Make the braids as needed for each project.

1. Choose three trims such as rattail and/or cordings.

2. Cut them to the lengths indicated in the patterns.

3. Tie them together at one end.

4. Braid them for the length needed.

5. Tie the ends in an overhand knot to make a tassel. Fluff the ends and trim evenly.

Patch the Panels

1. Make two tracings of the panel patterns and fasten them together to make one entire panel. Cut out the pattern.

2. Work Confetti Piecing sufficient for ten panels.

3. Using the pattern, cut 10 from each of the following: Confetti piece, muslin and backing fabric.

4. Place one muslin piece on the back of each Confetti piece. Place the backing and Confetti piece right sides together and sew around, leaving the upper edge open.

5. Turn and press. Topstitch using quilting thread in one color.

6. Using quilting thread in a second color, quilt each panel in the freeform pattern of your choice.

7. Add some tufts to each panel.

TOOLBOX

✓ Confetti Piecing, page 10
✓ Tufts, page 112
✓ Shower Curtain Topper Pattern, page 117
✓ Machine Quilting, page 141

Tufts

Tufts decorate some of the projects in this chapter. They are made from size 8 pearl cotton, but you may use other threads and fibers instead. Just make sure they are washable for items that will be washed.

You will need size 8 pearl cotton and a sturdy needle, such as a chenille needle.

1. Thread a chenille needle with one strand of pearl cotton and set it aside.

2. Wrap pearl cotton around your fingers until it is eight strands thick.

3. Take the needle and fasten it on the back of the work and stitch over the eight strands twice.

Confetti Piecing is enhanced by tufts, braided trim and quilting in a colorful thread.

4. Pulling the thread as tightly as you can without breaking it, tie the ends into a square knot. If it is necessary to finish off these ends, thread them into the chenille needle and take a stitch beginning at the base of the knot, then pull the ends between the layers of fabrics.

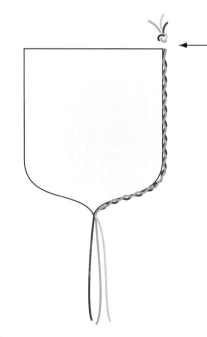

Diagram of the finished panel.

Make and Add the Braided Cording

1. To make the braided cording (first make one, and check on how long to cut the cordings in the beginning—you may need less or more), cut three cords each 30" long (you will need two sets per panel).

2. Tie the three cords together at one end. Make a braid 11" long (two for each panel).

3. Hand stitch the braid to one side of a panel, fastening it securely at each end. Trim off the knot.

4. Make a second braid for the other side of the panel and sew it on.

5. At the bottom of the panel, tie the two braids together in an overhand knot. Trim the tassel ends evenly. Repeat Steps 1 through 5 for each panel.

Make the Buttonhole Header

1. To make the buttonhole header, cut a strip 1¼" x 70½" from each of the following: the Confetti piece, muslin and backing fabric.

2. Cut the eyelet lace 105" long, narrow hem the short ends, and gather it.

3. Back the Confetti strip with the muslin strip and handle the two as one.

Diagram of the lace placement.

4. Place the gathered eyelet and the Confetti piece right sides together and pin.

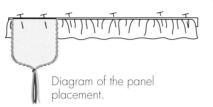

Diagram of the panel placement.

5. Arrange the panels on top of the lace and Confetti piece, right sides down, and pin.

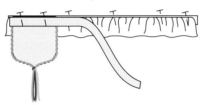

Diagram of the backing placement.

6. With right sides together, add the backing to the strip.

Sew the short end seams.

7. Sew the long seam and the short end seams.

8. Press the Confetti piece and the backing upward. Press the upper edges in ¼" and slipstitch.

9. Sew long buttonholes to match the placements of the shower curtain rings.

10. Topstitch and quilt the piece in the same manner as the panels.

11. Add some tufts to the strip.

12. To keep the panels hanging evenly, attach them to each other by hand stitching partway down the sides.

Lace Curtain Center

This is a project that will add a touch of color to a lace curtain. Use the same pattern as the Shower Curtain Topper, except place the top of the pattern on the fold of the fabric instead of having a top seam. These small, shaped tiebacks that accent the curtain panels are specially designed for smaller curtains.

Materials

- ¼ yd. lengths of 8 different 100 percent cotton quilting fabrics
- Cotton batting
- ¼ yd. of 100 percent cotton fabric for the backing
- Quilting thread in 2 colors*
- Pearl cotton thread, size 8
- 2 yd. each of 3 different purchased cordings or trims such as rattail or rayon cording (per panel)

*Used in this project: YLI Quilting Thread

(¼" seam allowance)

Patch the Panel Top

1. Make two tracings of the panel patterns and fasten them together to make one entire panel. Cut out the pattern.

2. Work Confetti Piecing sufficient for one panel.

Assemble the Panel

1. Using the pattern, cut one of each of the following: the Confetti piece, cotton batting and backing fabric.

2. Place batting on the back of the Confetti piece and handle the two as one.

3. With right sides together, add the backing and sew around, leaving an opening to turn.

4. Turn, press and slipstitch the opening closed.

5. Topstitch using quilting thread in one color.

6. Using quilting thread in a second color, quilt the header in the freeform pattern of your choice.

7. Add some tufts to the panel.

TOOLBOX

- ✓ Confetti Piecing, page 10
- ✓ Curtain Center Pattern, page 117
- ✓ Tufts, page 112
- ✓ Braided Trim, page 111
- ✓ Machine Quilting, page 141

fold

Diagram of the braid placement.

Make and Add the Braided Trim

1. To make two braids, cut the three cords each about 60" long.

2. Braid the cords.

3. Hand sew the braids, beginning and ending at the tassel locations.

4. Fold the header along the fold line and tie all of the tassel ends into one overhand knot. Trim the ends evenly.

Tieback for the Lace Curtains

Patch the Tieback Tops

1. Trace and cut out the pattern.

2. Work Confetti Piecing sufficient for two tiebacks.

Assemble the Tiebacks

1. Follow the instructions on the pattern, placing fabrics on the fold and cutting two of each of the following: Confetti piece, muslin and backing.

2. Place the muslin on back of each Confetti piece and handle the two as one.

3. With right sides together, add the backing to each Confetti piece and sew, leaving openings as indicated on the pattern.

4. Turn each to the right side through the top opening and press. Stitch this opening closed.

Materials

- ¼ yd. lengths of 100 percent cotton quilting fabrics in 8 different colors
- ¼ yd. muslin
- ¼ yd. of 100 percent cotton fabric for the backing
- Quilting thread in 2 colors*
- Pearl cotton thread, size 8
- 1½ yd. each of 3 different purchased cordings or trims such as rattail or rayon cording (per panel)

*Used in this project: YLI Quilting Thread

(¼" seam allowance)

TOOLBOX

✓ Confetti Piecing, page 10
✓ Tufts, page 112
✓ Braided Trim, page 111
✓ Backing, page 138
✓ Machine Quilting, page 141

Make and Add the Braided Trim

1. For each tieback, make two braids by cutting the three cords each about 25" long.

2. Braid the cords.

3. Sew the braids to the lower edges of the tieback, concealing the upper ends in the openings. Stitch the openings closed.

Finish the Tiebacks

1. Topstitch each tieback using quilting thread in one color.

2. Using quilting thread in a second color, quilt the tiebacks in the freeform pattern of your choice.

3. Add some tufts to each tieback.

4. Tie the tassel ends in overhand knots and trim the ends evenly.

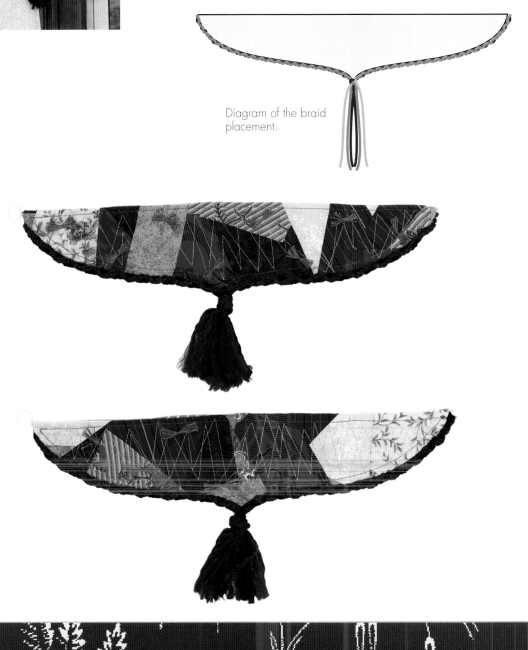

Diagram of the braid placement.

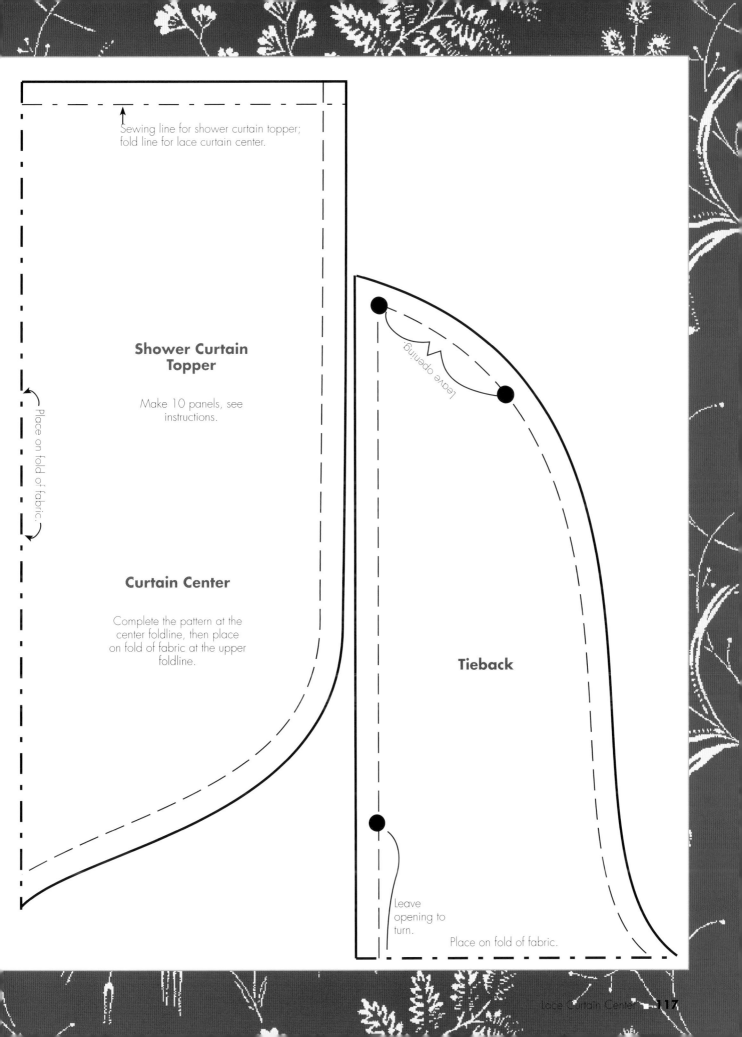

Shower Curtain Topper

Make 10 panels, see instructions.

Sewing line for shower curtain topper; fold line for lace curtain center.

Curtain Center

Complete the pattern at the center foldline, then place on fold of fabric at the upper foldline.

Place on fold of fabric.

Tieback

Leave opening.

Leave opening to turn.

Place on fold of fabric.

Matted Mirror Jewelry Holder

Materials

- Solid wood picture frame
- Paper
- Pencil
- Ruler
- ¼ yd. lengths of 100 percent cotton quilting fabrics in 8 different colors
- Muslin
- Mat board
- Batting
- Quilting thread
- Pearl cotton
- White glue
- Mirror to fit the frame
- Cardboard to fit the frame for the backing

The mat shown here is 6" x 14" with a 1¾" x 9½" opening for the mirror.

Make a quilted mat for a mirror and add some hooks for your favorite jewelry. Use a frame that is solid wood and thick enough to put hooks into.

TOOLBOX

✓ Confetti Piecing, page 10   ✓ Tufts, page 112   ✓ Machine Quilting, page 141

Make a Pattern to Fit Your Frame

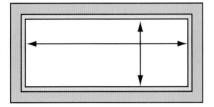

Measure the interior of the frame.

1. Make a pattern for the quilted mat by measuring the interior of the frame.

2. Cut a piece of paper this size.

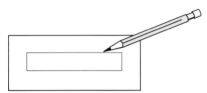

3. Decide on the dimensions of the mirror opening and mark it on the pattern.

4. Cut out the opening using the markings.

Patch the Mat

1. Using the cotton quilting fabrics, work Confetti Piecing.

2. Use the pattern to cut one from each of the following: Confetti piece and muslin, adding seam allowances of about 1" to the outer edge and the inner opening. Set the pattern aside.

3. Place the muslin on the back of the Confetti and handle the two as one.

4. Quilt the piece and add tufts.

Assemble the Pieces

1. Using the pattern, cut one of each of the following: mat board and batting.

2. Lightly glue the batting to the mat board. Allow to dry.

The back side of the mat board.

3. Place the quilted piece over the batting and begin gluing the outer edge on the back of the mat board. Work carefully to get the piece on evenly. Allow to dry.

4. With sharp scissors, trim almost to the inner corners diagonally, then fold the edges of the inner opening onto the mat board and glue.

5. Install the mat, mirror and cardboard backing in the frame and secure.

6. Drill holes for the hooks and screw in the hooks. Install hooks and wire or another type of hardware on the back of the frame for hanging.

Towel with Tabs

Materials

- Hand towel
- Small pieces of 100 percent cotton quilting fabrics
- Small piece of muslin
- Small piece of fabric for the backing
- 18" of shaded ribbon (¾" wide)
- Silk ribbons in floral colors and greens
- Quilting thread*
- Small piece of lightweight cardboard

*Used in this project: YLI quilting thread

(¼" seam allowance)

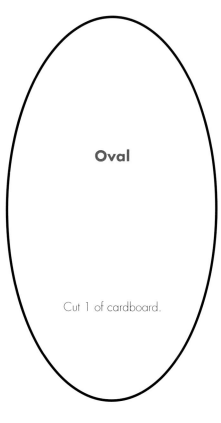

Oval

Cut 1 of cardboard.

A touch of silk ribbon embroidery makes this towel precious. Add some decorative tabs to make it a real conversation piece.

TOOLBOX

✓ Confetti Piecing, page 10   ✓ Machine Quilting, page 141

Patch the Tabs

1. Trace and cut out the tab pattern.

2. Using the cotton quilting fabrics, work Confetti Piecing to make enough for seven tabs and one oval motif.

Assemble and Attach the Tabs

1. Use the tab pattern to cut seven from each of the following: Confetti piece, muslin and backing.

2. Place one muslin on the back of each Confetti piece and handle the two as one.

3. Fold under and press the upper edges of the Confetti and backing pieces.

4. Place a Confetti piece and backing piece right sides together and sew the rounded edge, leaving the top unsewn. Turn and press.

5. Quilt each tab by hand or by machine.

6. Arrange the tabs evenly along the bottom edge of the towel.

7. Slipstitch the tabs to the towel.

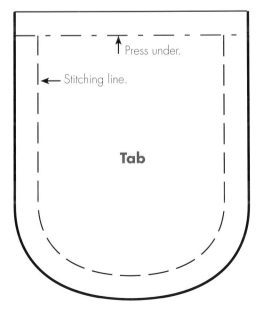

↑ Press under.

← Stitching line.

Tab

Make the Oval Motif

1. To make the oval motif, cut the oval pattern out of lightweight cardboard.

2. Cut a Confetti piece about ¼" larger than the cardboard pattern.

3. Using a dry iron, press the edges of the Confetti piece to the back of the cardboard.

4. Remove the cardboard and place the Confetti oval onto the towel, making sure it is centered and that the edges are tucked under neatly. Pin, then slipstitch all around.

5. Machine quilt along the seams and around the outer edge.

6. Tie a bow using the shaded ribbon.

7. Arrange and pin the bow to the edge of the motif. Hand stitch it in place.

8. Add some silk ribbon embroidery along the edges of the oval.

9. Embroider a small flower at the top of each tab.

Chairback Tote

Make several of these totes. You will find this to be a handy item. Use it for hair curlers, cosmetics, magazines or for whatever you need on-the-go. It is great for organizing! Hang it on hooks, pegs or the back of a chair.

Materials

- Paper
- Scissors
- Pencil
- Ruler
- ¼ yd. lengths of 100 percent cotton quilting fabrics in 8 different colors including fabric pieces for the bias binding and welting
- ¼ yd. of 100 percent cotton fabric for the handles
- Batting
- Cotton fabric for the backing (inside the bag and the back of the handles)
- Cotton quilting thread*
- Cotton welting cord
- 4 large buttons (optional)

*Used in this project: YLI cotton quilting thread

Cutting Instructions:

From the batting:
- Cut two from the pattern
- Cut one strip 27" x 3"
- Cut two strips 17" x 2½"

From the backing:
- Cut two from the pattern
- Cut one strip 27" x 3"
- Cut two strips 17" x 2½"

From the fabric for the handles:
- Cut two strips 17" x 2½"

(½" seam allowance)

Patch the Tote Pieces

1. Follow the diagram to make a full-size paper pattern.

2. Using the cotton quilting fabrics work Confetti Piecing sufficient for two pattern pieces and the 27" x 3" strip for the sides and bottom.

3. Using the pattern, cut two from the Confetti piece.

4. Make a stack of one backing, one batting and one Confetti for each section. Baste each together.

5. Quilt each section in the random quilting pattern of your choice.

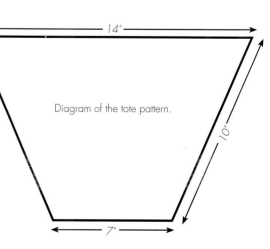

14"

Diagram of the tote pattern.

10"

7"

TOOLBOX

✓ Confetti Piecing, page 10
✓ Welting, page 143

✓ Bias Strips and Bias Binding, pages 138-139

✓ Machine Quilting, page 141

Make and Attach the Welting

1. Make two lengths of welting each 27" long.

2. Machine baste one to the bag front and the other to the bag back along the sides and bottoms (see photo for placement).

Assemble the Tote

1. Sew the 27" x 3" strip for the bottom and sides to the bag front through all layers.

2. Sew the bag back to the other long edge of the strip. Trim the welting even with the top of the bag.

3. Make bias binding 2⅛" wide.

4. Sew the binding over the seam allowances just made (inside the bag) and on the upper edge of the bag.

Neatly finish the inside of the bag with bias binding.

Diagram of the handle placement.

Make and Attach the Handles

1. Place one 17" x 2½" fabric strip and one 17" x 2½" backing strip right sides together, and place one 17" x 2½" batting piece on the back.

2. Sew around, leaving an opening to turn.

3. Trim, turn and press. Slipstitch the opening closed.

4. Repeat Steps 1 through 3 to make the second handle.

5. Machine sew one handle to each side of the bag, stitching a square pattern with an X inside it.

Finish the Tote

1. About 1½" above the bag, place welting cord onto the backing of the handle and wrap the handle so the side edges meet.

2. Hand stitch the side edges together leaving the final 1½" free. Trim the ends of the cording so they won't show.

3. Sew on four buttons, if desired.

Faux Crazy Floorcloth

Finished size: 19" x 28½"

Add some color to a room with a "faux crazy" floorcloth. Here are basic instructions for making a floorcloth. To pursue the art of painting canvas further, choose a book on the subject. One is listed in the Recommended Reading section on page 144.

Materials

- Hemmed piece of heavy canvas
- Gesso
- Fine sandpaper
- Off white exterior latex paint
- Acrylic paints in colors of your choice
- Paint brushes
- Painter's masking tape (if needed)
- Water-based polyurethane
- Clear butcher's or bowling alley wax

Prepare the Canvas

1. Pour some gesso into a container and add water to thin it.

2. Paint the thinned gesso mixture on the canvas. Let it dry, then paint a coat of unthinned gesso. Let dry.

3. If the canvas feels rough, sand it smooth.

4. Apply one or two layers of exterior paint and let dry thoroughly after each coat.

Paint the Crazy Quilted Design

1. Choose a design by sketching on a sheet of paper or directly onto the canvas. Make the design of your choice, or use a design similar to the one shown here.

2. Begin to paint. Add a touch of water to the acrylic paints if needed so they spread on easily. Here are some techniques to try (try them first on a sheet of paper):

- Using a stencil brush and very small amounts of paint, dab paint onto a previously painted color.
- Use a very fine brush to make stripes or curlicues.
- Use masking tape to make even lines or to prevent painting on previously painted areas.
- Make polka dots freehand. Outline everything in a light grey (suggests shadows), dark grey or black.

3. When the painting is finished, allow to dry thoroughly.

4. Paint on one or two coats of polyurethane. Allow to dry after each coat.

5. Using a rag, cover the surface with a light coat of wax. Go back over the wax with a clean, dry rag and buff it.

6. You may want to add a rubber coating to the back if it is to be used on a smooth floor.

Raggy Bathmat

This mix of materials makes a wonderfully absorbent bathmat. It will add lots of character to your bathroom!

Materials

- ¼ yd. lengths of 100 percent cotton quilting fabrics in 8 different colors
- Old bath towel
- ⅓ yd. of 100 percent cotton fabric for the raggy trim
- ¼ yd. of 100 percent cotton fabric for the binding

TOOLBOX

✓ Confetti Piecing, page 10   ✓ Raggy Trim, page 126   ✓ Bias Strips and Bias Binding, pages 138-139

Patch the Bath Mat Top

1. Choose the finished size of your bathmat. The standard size is 20" x 28", but you can make it any size to fit your bathroom.

2. Use the cotton quilting fabrics to work Confetti Piecing to this size.

Add the Towel Backing

1. Cut a piece of the towel using the same measurements.

2. Baste the towel and Confetti piece wrong sides together.

Make and Add the Raggy Trim

1. Make raggy trim.

2. Sew meandering lines of raggy trim on the Confetti piece, making them close enough to quilt the layers of the mat.

Make and Add the Bias Binding

1. Cut strips 2⅛" wide for the binding around the bath mat.

2. Sew the strips together to make a length sufficient to go around the mat.

3. Place the binding strip right-side down on the wrong side of one edge of the mat. Sew using ½" seam allowance.

4. Press and fold to the front.

5. Fold in the raw edge and edge stitch.

Raggy Trim

This trim makes use of the raw edges of cotton fabric. Excess threads come loose in the wash and the edges fluff.

Note: Use the lengthwise or crosswise grain of the fabric, not a bias cut.

1. Cut two strips 1½" wide and place them together.

2. Press them in half lengthwise.

Sew along the crease.

3. To sew raggy trim to a project, sew along the crease.

4. After sewing, make snips about ¼" apart and up to approximately ⅛" of the stitching.

5. Wash and dry the project, then trim away any clumps or excess threads.

Whimsy Starfish Bellpull

Finished size: 4¾" x 24" (not including the tassel)

The cording used to edge the sections of this bellpull is made of a fuzzy novelty yarn.

Materials

- ¼ yd. lengths of 100 percent cotton quilting fabrics in 8 different colors
- ¼ yd. cotton organdy fabric or interfacing
- ¼ yd. cotton fabric for the backing
- 4 yd. cording
- 24 starfish brass charms
- Quilting thread*
- 8 buttons
- Bone ring
- Tassel (purchased or self-made)

*Used in this project: YLI Quilting Thread

(¼" seam allowance)

Patch the Bellpull Pieces

1. Trace and cut out the pattern.

2. Using the cotton quilting fabrics, work Confetti Piecing sufficient for eight pattern pieces.

Assemble the Bellpull

1. Using the pattern, cut eight from each of the following: the Confetti piece, cotton organdy and backing.

2. Place an organdy piece on the back of each Confetti piece and handle the two as one.

3. Place the backing on the Confetti piece right sides together. Sew around, leaving an opening to turn.

4. Turn and press. Hand stitch cording around the entire outer edge of each piece, concealing the ends in the opening.

5. Stitch the opening closed.

6. By machine, freehand quilt each section of the bellpull.

7. Line up the sections and hand stitch them together.

TOOLBOX

✓ Confetti Piecing, page 10
✓ A Basic Tassel, page 142
✓ Cordings, page 139
✓ Backing, page 138
✓ Machine Quilting, page 141

Add Embellishments

1. Hand stitch a charm to the lower corners of each section.

2. Sew a button to each.

3. Fasten the tassel to the bottom of the bellpull, embellishing it with charms.

4. Sew a bone ring to the upper back for hanging.

To make a similar tassel, combine wool, cotton and rayon chenille yarns. Wrap for about 1" with the cotton yarn. Then pull out the wool yarns and tie them neatly in knots all around. Tie some charms to the long strands of the tassel.

Whimsy Starfish Bellpull

Leave opening for turning.

Pippi, A Doll

Creating a doll using Confetti Piecing is another way to use crazy quilting in your home décor. Pippi wears her Confetti-pieced sundress over striped bloomers, leather sandals and a band-aid on one knee. Her braided orange hair is made of pearl cotton and is tied with fabric scraps matching her bloomers.

She is about 25" tall standing. Her head is 2½" from chin to top. She is made of white muslin painted with acrylic paints.

Created by trial and error stitching, her face has a seam down the center of it to give the details of a profile—chin, nose and forehead. Her neck is a separate piece. Her arms and legs are each made in two sections and joined by stitches. Making the limbs in sections allows her to be posed in a certain way—in this case, as a sitting doll, by stitching the limbs into position.

I didn't know why her face was tilted upwards (no matter what I did, this could not be changed) until I was struck by the idea of making her a butterfly net. The butterfly in her hair was then so obvious an idea it was hardly a thought. Sweet irony!

See Recommended Reading on page 144 for an excellent book on creating dolls.

The Stained Glass Method of Crazy Quilting

This method works well with flannel fabrics that seem to stay in place nicely on the foundation. The edges of patches are butted together, eliminating the bulk of seams, and covered with bias binding. You will need flannel for patching, muslin for the foundation and cotton fabric for making the bias strips. *Note:* Cut the patches with rounded edges.

Pin the patches to the muslin foundation.

Sew the bias binding.

1. Cut a rounded patch to fit into a corner.

2. Place the corner patch on a corner.

3. To butt the patches together, lay the second patch so the edge of it is under the first patch.

4. Cut along the edge of the first fabric so it butts up against the second patch. Remove the excess.

5. Pin each patch as it is laid. There is no need to baste (unless you want to) since the flannel holds onto the muslin. Continue until the block is completely covered.

6. To make the bias binding, cut strips 1⅛" wide (no need to sew them together). Be sure to cut plenty of strips because you will need a lot of bias binding.

7. Press under both long edges of the strips to make finished pieces that are a full ½" wide (or a hair more).

8. One patch at a time, machine sew one folded edge of bias binding along the curved edge of the patch.

9. Press the binding down onto the adjoining patch and leave the open edge unsewn for now.

10. When all the patch edges are covered, slipstitch the open edges of the bias through all layers.

Note: You can follow-up by machine edge stitching along both edges of each piece of bias (optional).

Child's Cuddle Quilt

Bright and colorful (and soft and cozy) flannel fabrics are united in the Stained Glass Method of crazy quilting. This is a child's carry-around quilt, not a bed quilt. It's perfect for storytime or for snuggling up to watch a movie. Every kid needs one! *Note:* If the quilt is used for an infant, eliminate the ties and quilt it instead.

Materials

- Tracing paper
- Pencil
- 2 yd. muslin
- Pieces of bright, solid color fabrics (flannel or smooth cotton)
- ½ yd. each of 5 or more colorful cotton flannel fabrics
- 1¼ yd. plain cotton flannel for the borders
- 1 yd. plain cotton for the bias bindings
- 1½ yd. 100 percent cotton fabric for the backing
- High-loft poly batting
- Bright colored pearl cotton thread

Cutting Instructions

From the muslin:
- Cut eight 12" squares.

From the plain flannel:
- Cut four pieces 7" x 34" for the borders.

From the printed flannel:
- Cut four 7" squares for the corner blocks.

TOOLBOX

✓ The Stained Glass Method of Crazy Quilting, page 131

✓ Bias Strips and Bias Binding, pages 138-139

✓ Appliqué, page 138
✓ Tie the Quilt, page 143

Diagram of the quilt layout.

Assemble the blocks into columns.

Cut the Triangle Foundation Pieces

1. Cut two of the 12" muslin squares in half diagonally to make four triangular pieces.

2. Cut one of the 12" muslin squares in quarters diagonally to make four smaller triangular pieces.

3. Trace the appliqués and cut them out. *Note:* On the patterns, some seam allowances must be added. Add ¼" all around as you cut.

Make the Appliqué Blocks

1. Place a bright solid flannel or smooth cotton fabric patch (larger than the appliqué) in the center of each of the 12" square blocks.

2. Press the outer edges of the appliqués under ¼".

3. Pin the appliqués to the solid fabric patch centered in the 12" squares and slipstitch all around.

Patch and Assemble the Blocks

1. Patch the appliquéd blocks and the remaining square and triangular muslin blocks following instructions for the Stained Glass Method.

2. Place the blocks in order on the floor or other large surface, as shown in the diagram.

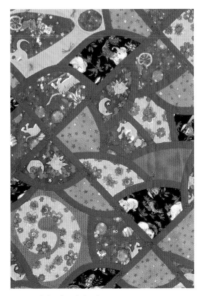

Assemble the blocks.

3. Join the blocks into columns using bias binding and the same method of sewing, then slipstitching the bias.

4. Join the columns, continuing in the same method.

5. Join two plain flannel 7½" side borders with binding using the the same method.

6. Attach a 7½" x 7½" corner block to each end of each of the remaining border pieces.

Attach the Borders

1. Attach the remaining borders.

2. Cut out six appliqués for the borders.

3. Slipstitch two appliqués to each border piece.

Attach the border pieces.

Finish the Quilt

1. Cut the batting the same size as the quilt top.

2. Cut the backing the same size as the quilt top.

3. Stack the backing, batting and quilt top. Baste.

4. Make bias binding.

5. Apply the bias binding around the outer edges of the quilt.

6. Tie the quilt using the pearl cotton threads.

Pillow

Make a soft and cozy pillow with decorative tabs to match the quilt.

Materials

- ½ yd. muslin for the foundation
- ¼ yd. flannel for the tabs
- ½ yd. cotton for the backing
- Small pieces of colorful cotton flannel for the patches
- ½ yd. plain cotton fabric for the bias binding
- 12" pillow form

Cutting Instructions

From the muslin:
- Cut one 13" square for the foundation.

From the cotton:
- Cut one 13" square for the backing.

(½" seam allowance)

Patch the Square

Patch the muslin square following instructions for the Stained Glass Method.

Make the Tabs

1. Trace and cut out the tab pattern.

2. Using the tab pattern, cut 32 from the flannel fabric.

3. To make the tabs, sew the upper edges of two tabs together. Trim, turn and press. Repeat for the remaining tabs (you will have 16 total tabs when finished).

4. Place four tabs along each edge of the pillow top and baste.

Assemble the Pillow

1. To make the backing, sew the 13" cotton square to the pillow top right sides together, leaving a large opening to insert a pillow form.

2. Turn the pillow cover right-side out.

3. Insert the pillow form.

4. Slipstitch the opening closed.

TOOLBOX

✓ The Stained Glass Method of Crazy Quilting, page 131
✓ Bias Strips and Bias Binding, pages 138-139
✓ Tab pattern, page 135

Swirl

Seam allowances included.

Star

Add seam allowance
when cutting fabric.

Moon

Add seam allowance
when cutting fabric.

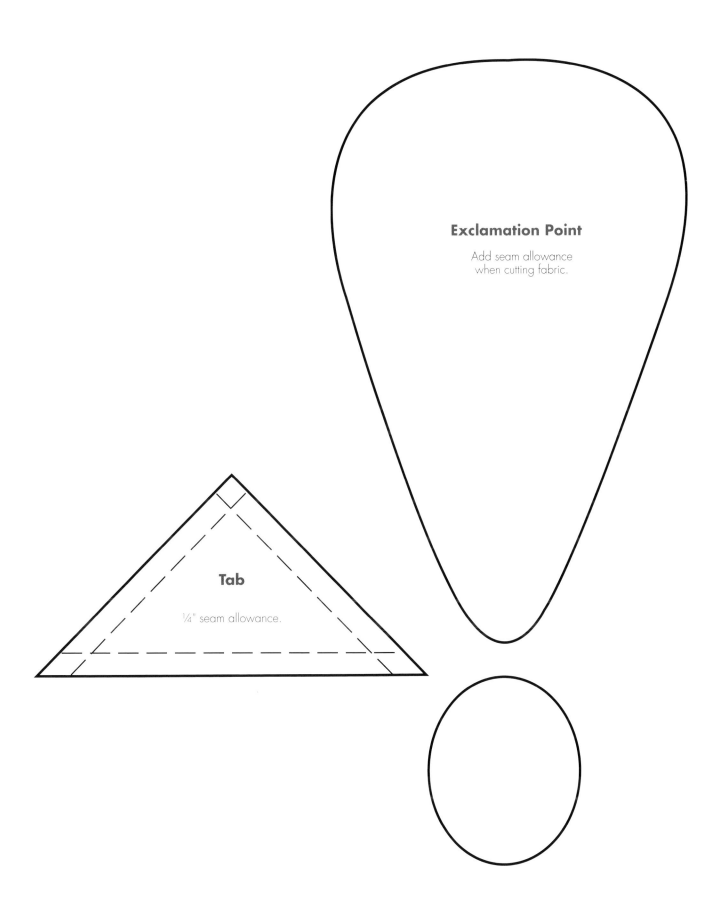

Exclamation Point

Add seam allowance
when cutting fabric.

Tab

¼" seam allowance.

Glossary

Appliqué

A cut-out shape sewn onto a background fabric.

1. Cut a pattern out of paper.
2. Cut a piece of fabric adding seam allowances of ⅛" to ¼".
3. Place the paper pattern on the back of the fabric.
4. Press the fabric's seam allowance onto the paper pattern.
5. Remove the paper and pin the fabric piece onto the background fabric.
6. Slipstitch the fabric piece onto the background fabric.

Backing

The fabric used for the underside of a project.

1. Place the backing and top piece right sides together and pin.

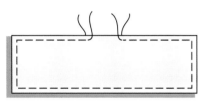

Sew the backing to the top piece.

2. Sew around, leaving an opening to turn.
3. Trim the seams if necessary. Often it is helpful to trim diagonally across corners so the corners turn nicely. Turn right-side out. Press so the edges lie smoothly.
4. Slipstitch the opening closed.

Add trims to the edge of the right side of the backing fabric.

Note: If adding trims into the seam, pin, then baste the trim to the right side of the piece, matching the trim's seam allowance to that of the project. Finish the ends in a way that is appropriate for the trim. Then continue attaching the backing to the project as usual.

Bandings

Long, narrow pieces of crazy quilting.
Patching bandings using the Antique Method of Crazy Quilting and the Top-stitch Appliqué method is easy because there is much less "puzzle" over how to add the next patch.

Note: Bandings can be made into bellpulls or curtain tiebacks, or can be used to decorate larger things such as pillows and draperies. Coil bandings into baskets and chair cushions.

Beading

Adding beads to enhance and embellish projects by sewing them on or by adding beaded fringes.

1. To sew on beads, use beading thread and a needle that will go through the beads. A fine sewing needle often works, but you may wish to use a beading needle.
2. It is often a good idea to sew through each bead twice to secure it well to the fabric.
3. Sew them on one at a time or string two or three on the needle to make a small cluster.
Note: Some bead finishes may not hold up to washing. Test them before using them in a washable project.

Beaded Fringe

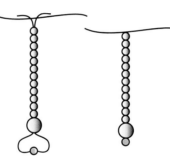

To make a beaded fringe, you will need beads, a beading needle and beading thread. Begin with a sizeable quantity of beads. Purchase seed beads in hanks (which are the long strings of beads that they are sold by) or in large quantity packages. You may wish to use several sizes of beads in a fringe. Use a beading needle so you can string a few beads at a time. I like to use size 11 seed beads for fringe, sometimes adding larger seed beads or 4mm glass beads.

1. Secure the beading thread well into the fabric and test it to be sure it holds.
2. String on the length of beads needed for the fringe, plus one more bead.
3. Missing the final bead, run the needle up through all of the remaining beads.
4. Make one or two stitches at the top of the fringe.
5. Run the needle through the fabric to the next fringe placement.

Looped Fringe

1. Fasten beading thread onto the fabric.
2. String on one beginning bead, then the remaining beads for the loop.
3. Go back through the beginning bead and into the fabric.
4. Run the needle through the fabric to the next bead placement.

Bias Strips and Bias Binding

Used for making ruffles or for covering the raw edges of a project.

1. Begin with a square or rectangle of fabric. Fold it in half diagonally.
2. With the rotary cutter and straight-edge, trim away the folded edge.

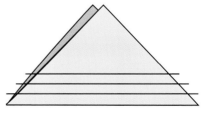

Cut the strips for the binding on the diagonal.

3. Measure and cut the widths of strips needed.
• To bind a ½" wide seam:
 Cut the bias 2⅛" wide.
 Sew with a ½" seam allowance.
• To bind a ¼" wide seam:
 Cut the bias 1⅛" wide.
 Sew with a ¼" seam allowance.

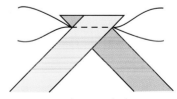

Sew strips together to make longer strips.

4. Sew the strips together to obtain the length needed. Press the seams open.
5. To apply bias binding, sew it to the project right sides together.
6. Press the bias binding to the back.

7. Fold in the raw edge and slipstitch over the seam.

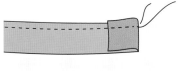

Notes:
- To sew bias binding around something where ends meet, fold the bias strip inward about ½". Sew around, then overlap the end about ½" on the fold. This makes a neatly finished end that can then be slipstitched if desired.
- To bind a square or rectangular shape, sew then slipstitch the binding to the side edges, making the binding even with top and bottom of the piece. Then bind the top and bottom edges, sewing on the binding so it is about ½" longer at both sides. Fold the ends in neatly while slipstitching.

Circle Pattern

A paper pattern in a circular shape.

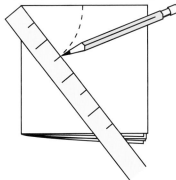

1. Fold a sheet of paper in fourths.
2. Using pencil and ruler, measure one half of the diameter of the circle (if it is a 16" circle, measure 8") from the point of the fold outward.
3. Measure and mark until you have a line that you can easily follow.
4. Cut along the pencil line.
5. Unfold the paper.

Cordings

Lengths of fibers made to trim and add detail to projects.

Sew-On Cordings
1. Meander and couch cordings or other trims onto a patch. Do this before or after the patch is sewn down.
2. Conceal cord endings under adjoining patches or knot the ends and leave them free.

Self-Made Cordings

It is easy to make your own cordings. Opt for some interesting fibers and design what you need when you need it, adding original touches to your projects. Use cordings to embellish a patch, make hanging cords for tassels or to edge a project. You will need a twisting device (a pencil or a cord twister), a holder (a bench vise, hook or door knob), a weight and the fibers. A crank-style cord twister is worth having. It works better than a pencil and is quicker. For an even twist, use a weight. See Resources on page 144 for Cord Twister and Corder Weight.

Note: When learning to make your own cording, begin with about a yard of fiber. The finished length will vary according to the fibers used, but it will be somewhere less than half of what you began with. The greatest length of cord you can make depends on how well you can reach the center. This may be about three yards or so of fiber length before twisting. You must be able to reach the center and place the weight, and then hold it up so it can twist. It takes only one fiber to make a cord. However, combining two or more different fibers creates different textures and thicknesses. Experiment!

1. Knot the fiber and fasten it to a hook or doorknob. Place a pencil (or use a cord twister) in the other end and twist in one direction. Twist until you feel the cord becoming tight. If you twist too far, knots will form on the cord. Simply untwist until the knots disappear.

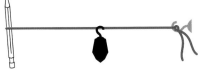

2. After twisting the fiber, place a weight in the center.

3. Bring the two ends together (the one on the pencil or twister and the one on the hook) and allow the cord to twist. Knot the two ends together.

Couch/Couching
An embroidery stitch that fastens a fiber onto the surface of fabric by stitching over it. Note: It can be done by hand (see Couching under Embroidery Stitches) or machine. By machine, use a zigzag stitch with the needle plunking down on each side of the material being couched.

Edge Stitch
Machine sew right next to the folded edge of a fabric.

Fabrications
Here are a few ways to add interest, texture and dimension to your projects made of the Topstitch Applique and Antique Methods of Crazy Quilting. Prepare some patches ahead of time or as you need them.

Checkerboarding
Fabrics sewn in a checkerboard pattern.
1. Sew strips of fabrics together and press.
2. Cut this piece into strips, cutting perpendicular to the stripes.
3. Sew the new strips together to create a checkerboard effect.

Fabric Fringes
Fringes made by unravelling fabric. Note: Use decorator fabric with substantial threads. Pull out the lighter threads to leave the heavier (threads are often fine in one direction and heavier in the other).
1. Fold a piece of fabric in half lengthwise.
2. Ravel the two open edges up to within a seam allowance.
3. Zigzag along the folded edge to prevent further raveling.

Flange
An edge of cloth used as an embellishment, such as under the folded edge of a patch.
1. Cut a strip of fabric on the bias about 1½" wide.
2. Fold the strip in half lengthwise and press.
3. Place it under the folded patch edge so it peeks out about ⅛", then topstitch the patch.

Flanges make neat edgings for patches.

Embroidery Stitches

Here are some basic stitches to get you started. For more stitches and for variations and ways to use them, refer to "The Magic of Crazy Quilting."

Blanket Stitch

Make this stitch in either direction- left or right. Stitch vertically with the thread under the needle. Pull through and repeat. End with a short tacking stitch.

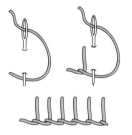

Bullion Stitch

Begin by making a stitch but do not pull through. Wrap the thread around the needle enough times to equal the length of the stitch. Hold the wraps in place, and pull the needle through. Sink the needle where the stitch began, and give a little tug to settle the wraps in place.

Chain Stitch

Make this stitch in either direction- left or right. Stitch horizontally with the thread under the needle. Pull through and repeat. End with a short tacking stitch.

Coral Stitch

Make a short slanting stitch with the thread going over, then under the needle. Snug up the thread, and pull through. Repeat, working towards the left. To work towards the right, wrap the thread in the opposite direction.

Couching

Use couching for fibers that cannot be pulled through the fabric. Fasten on the thread or fiber to be couched, or secure its ends under patches. With a second thread, make a short tacking stitch over the couched thread and through the fabric.

Cretan Stitch

Working downwards and keeping the needle horizontal, first make a stitch to the right of an imaginary line, and then to the left. Repeat.

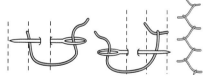

Feather Stitch

Working downwards along an imaginary line, make a slanting stitch first to one side of the line and then the other. Repeat.

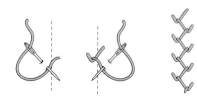

Double Feather Stitch

Same as the Feather stitch, but make an extra stitch at each side of the line.

French Knot

Wrap the thread around the needle following the direction shown. Snug up the thread then pull through the fabric next to where the thread first came through. Vary the stitch by wrapping two, three, or more times.

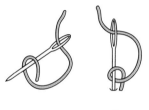

Lazy Daisy

Stitch with the thread under the needle, and pull through. Repeat. End with a short tacking stitch.

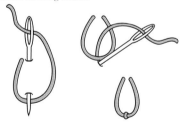

Outline Stitch

Stitch toward the right having the needle facing left. Make stitches immediately next to each other, or farther apart to make a narrower line.

Pintucks

Pleats sewn in place on fabric.

1. Iron pleats into a piece of fabric then edge stitch the creases.

2. Press all in the same direction.

Note: Vary the recipe by sewing perpendicular to the pintucks, first one direction then the other. This turns the tucks in the direction you are sewing.

Scrunching Fabrics

The effect achieved by holding fabric scrunches in place with ties, stitches or beads.

Fitting

Done by either making a paper pattern (see Paper Patterns below), or by measuring.

1. To fit by measuring, use a tape measure to accurately find the dimensions.

2. Sketch the furniture or window on a sheet of paper and write in the dimensions.

3. Decide how much you want to add for any or all of the following: ease or fullness, header or rod pocket, hems and/or any extra length.

Note: If you are not sure, then sew the item using a cheap fabric. Get the fabric to fit the way you want it to, then use it for your pattern.

Gathering

Used to make ruffles, gathering pulls up a length of lace, eyelet lace, ribbon, trim or fabric to fit onto another flat piece.

Note: A short piece of lightly gathered lace needs only one line of gathering thread. Use two lines (or more) for wider laces and ruffles.

1. Sew a line of machine basting along the seam line.

2. Sew the second line of machine basting within the seam allowance.

3. Pull up on both ends of the gathering thread(s). Or, knot one end and pull up on the other.

4. Pull and spread the gathers along until the ruffle fits the piece it is intended for.

5. Pin, and baste or sew the gathered piece to the project.

Hand Stitching

When machine stitching is not practical, or if a hand-stitched look is preferred.

1. Begin and end with several tiny stitches close together instead of knots.

2. Use a single thread and a fine needle such as a size 12 Sharp.

3. Make stitches small and as invisibly as possible. See Slipstitching below.

Interface, Interfacing

An extra layer of fabric that can either act as a stiffener, give extra body or add stability.

Note: Use muslin, batiste, cotton organdy or any commercial interfacing.

Machine Quilting

Used with the Confetti Piecing method to stabilize the seams and layers, and is decorative as well.

1. Choose a thread color that enhances the fabric colors.

2. Set the machine at a long stitch length.

3. Use a quilting or other sharp needle appropriate for the fabrics, and a regular foot or an embroidery foot.

4. Use an ordinary sewing thread in the bobbin that matches or blends with the back of the project.

5. Assemble the project's layers as they will be when finished.

6. Pin, then baste to hold the layers while stitching.

7. Quilt in straight lines or meander at will to create freeform patterns. Run the machine at a slow speed while you maneuver the project.

8. Any ends that are on the project that are not at its edges should be brought to the back and tied. Thread them into a hand sewing needle and bring them between the layers to finish off completely.

Paper Patterns

Patterns created using paper.

You will need newspaper, scissors, and sometimes tape, a pencil and a ruler.

1. Tape together sheets of newspaper as needed.

2. Place the newspaper on the furniture.

3. Crease to indicate edges, then cut along the creases. Check that it fits. If not, make the necessary changes.

4. Get the pattern just right: any flaws will likely show up in the finished piece. Fold it in half to make sure both sides match.

Check that any rounded corners match. Be sure to add any seam allowances as you cut fabrics. If the piece you are making will be padded (batting), consider adding an extra inch all around in case the piece "takes up" in the finishing.

Paper Piecing of Fans

The easiest and most accurate way to make pieced fans.

Note: Use artists tracing paper for lightweight fabrics and 20 lb. computer paper for heavier fabrics.

1. Trace the number of fan patterns needed onto the tracing paper, or photocopy as many as needed onto the computer paper.

2. Cut out the tracings or photocopies. As you cut and sew the blades, add seam allowances at the outer edges.

3. Precut fabric pieces for the blades of the fan, making them slightly larger than the pattern pieces.

4. Stack the first two blades right sides together.

5. Lay the paper with pencil lines or printing facing up over the two fabrics.

6. Place the seam line of the first two blades where the seam will be on the fabrics. Pin.

7. Sew the seam, sewing a little into the area of the fan's center (¼" to ½" or so).

8. Turn the piece over and trim the seam allowance evenly. Press the second fan blade open.

9. Continue, adding one blade at a time until all are sewn on. Keep the paper pattern in place.

10. Trim outer edges evenly leaving a seam allowance.

11. Press the upper edge of the fan to the back along the seam line.

12. Cut out a fan center adding seam allowances all around. Press under the upper seam allowance.

13. On the papered side of the fan, put in two or three pins to indicate the placement of the fan center.

14. Turn the paper so the pieced fan is right-side up, and place the center according to the pins.

15. Pin, then slipstitch in place.

16. Remove the sewn paper after the center is sewn.

Quilting

See "Machine Quilting."

Right Sides Together

By joining two pieces with their right sides facing, the seam allowances, or raw edges, will finish up on the wrong side of the piece.

Rod Pocket

A strip of fabric sewn to the upper back of a quilt to use it as a wallhanging (or the top of a fabric panel to use it as a curtain).

1. Cut a strip of fabric about 6" wide by the width of the quilt.

2. Turn under each end ¼" twice and stitch.

3. Fold in and press the long edges under ¼" to ½" and pin.

4. Slipstitch the strip to the quilt backing (stitches do not go through to the front).

5. Slide a dowel or curtain rod through the pocket and hang.

Seam Allowance

The distance from the edge of the fabric to the sewn seam.

Note: To obtain an even seam allowance, use markings on your machine's presser foot or on the bed of the machine. If there is no marking to follow, measure from the point of the needle and apply a piece of masking tape. I try to use a ½" seam allowance wherever possible. But for smaller projects, ¼" is often better. Larger allowances are often trimmed after sewing. Instructions may say "stay within the seam allowance," so "the stitching" specified will not show on the right side after the seam is sewn.

Slipstitching

Stitching by hand that is done so stitches won't show.

Note: Slipstitching is often used for stitching up openings left when a piece is sewn right sides together, then turned right-side out. The same stitch is used for appliqué.

1. Use a single thread and a size 12 Sharp needle.

2. Fasten on the thread, then take a short stitch through one fabric, then a few threads of the other. Pull through and repeat.

Stabilize/Stabilizer

A purchased product, plain computer paper or artist's tracing paper that is used when machine sewing puckers.

Note: Commercially, there are stabilizers that iron-away, wash-away or can be torn away. Try a few types and settle on whatever works for you.

Stitch-in-the-Ditch

A second sewing on top of a previously sewn seam that is sometimes used for quilting.

Tassels

Threads bound together at one end used to embellish projects.

There are as many ways to make tassels as there are fibers to make them out of. Like cordings, make tassels out of novelty yarns, embroidery materials and even silk ribbons.

You can use them in many ways; hang them from bellpulls, lampshades or the corners of pillows, afghans and slipcovers. Some tassels are not washable, especially the Really Fancy Decorator Tassels (see below). But you can still fasten them onto a washable project. Sew a piece of hook and loop tape or a large snap fastener to the hanging cord and to the project. Simply remove it for washing!

A Basic Tassel

1. Make a hanging cord (see cordings on page 139). Knot the ends together.

2. Begin with the fibers of your choice and a piece of cardboard the size of the tassel. Wrap the fibers around the cardboard until it is the thickness desired.

3. Cut through the fibers on the cardboard and open them out flat.

4. Place the center of the fibers about 1" above the knot of the hanging cord. Take some thread or any strong fiber and wrap tightly at this point, then tie off. Bring the fibers of the tassel downwards.

5. Thread a sturdy needle with a long length of one of the tassel fibers.

6. Hold the beginning end along with the tassel fibers, then wrap the tassel just above the knot of the hanging cord.

7. Sew through the wrappings several times, then run the needle down through and cut the end even with the bottom of the tassel.

Chinese Knot Tassel

1. First , make the knotted top following the diagram. Chinese knots are woven; first make the loops as shown, then weave the cord end through.

2. Adjust the loops so they are even and make sure the cord ends are aligned.

3. Use cording for the knotted top or make covered welting (see page 143).

4. Cut a piece of cardboard the length desired.

5. Wrap the fiber of your choice around the cardboard until it is the thickness desired.

6. Cut at the bottom of the cardboard. Open out the fibers and hold the center of them about 1" above the lower end of the Chinese knot.

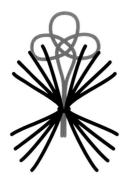

7. Wrap tightly using thread and fasten off.

8. Bring the fiber ends down and wrap again about ½" below the first knot using the color or fiber of your choice.

Really Fancy Decorator Tassels

Really elaborate tassels are beyond the scope of this book.

Some special supplies are needed including tassel tape and a means of making bullion fringe. These supplies are available in a kit (see the Resources on page 144).

Wooden Bead Tassel

1. Choose a wooden bead that has a large enough hole to pull fibers up through. Paint or apply a finish to the bead.

2. Make a hanging cord (see cordings on page 139).

3. Wrap a piece of cardboard with the tassel fibers.

4. Place the hanging cord under the fibers on the cardboard, then knot the ends together.

5. Remove the fibers from the cardboard by cutting or sliding them.

6. Bring the hanging cord up through the bead and tie a knot at the top of the bead. If needed, place some glue inside the bead to hold the fibers in place.

Tie the Quilt

Ties made on front or back to hold layers together.

1. Use pearl cotton, silk ribbon or the fibers of your choice.

2. Place the quilt on a flat surface, then baste or safety-pin throughout.

3. Thread a heavy needle with the fiber you are using and take a small stitch.

4. Cut the thread and tie the ends in a square knot.

5. Make enough ties to secure the layers. I often make them about 4" to 6" apart.

Topstitch

Similar to edge stitching, but done ¼" or so in from the edge.

Trim, Turn and Press

A standard procedure in assembling many projects.

1. Trim wide seam allowances back to about ¼".

2. Lop corners diagonally so they turn nicely.

3. Clip curved seams almost to the seam allowance and make a triangle shape if the seam curves outwards.

4. Turn the object right-side out.

5. Press to flatten the seams. Apply steam if needed, or lay a damp press cloth on while pressing. Press on a padded surface to retain the integrity of any embellishments that have been applied.

Welting

A covered cord that is sewn into a seam used to provide a classy and neat finish to many projects.

1. Purchase cotton filler cord. This is available in several thicknesses. I used a thickness of ³⁄₁₆" for most of the projects in this book.

2. Cut bias strips of fabric equivalent to the diameter of the cord plus two seam allowances.

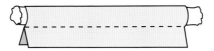

3. Using a zipper foot, sew the bias onto the cord using a long machine stitch. Do not stitch right next to the cord.

4. Sew the welting to the project with a regular machine stitch and sewing closer to the cord than previously (this keeps the previous stitching from showing).

5. Where the two ends of the cording come together, push the fabric back and trim so the ends butt rather than overlap.

6. Cross the ends of the fabric and sew over them.

Welting, Covered

Welting that is not sewn into a seam.
Note: This type of welting is used for the Chinese Knot Tassels (see page 142).

1. Purchase cotton filler cord. Do not cut the filler cord.

2. Cut bias strips of fabric equivalent to the diameter of the cord plus two seam allowances.

3. Measure along the cord for the length needed.

4. Begin sewing on the bias fabric at this point, going away from the beginning of the cord. Sew so the fabric is not tight to the cording.

5. Stitch the fabric to the cord where you began sewing.

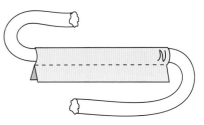

6. Trim the excess seam allowance.

7. Dampen your fingers and push on the fabric at the end stitched to the filler cord (you will be gradually turning it right side out). Keep pushing slowly (don't force it) until the bias fabric covers to the beginning of the cord.

Resources

American Frame Corporation
Arrowhead Park
400 Tomahawk Dr.
Maumee, OH 43537
(800) 537-0944
http://www.americanframe.com
Picture frames

Dharma Trading Co.
P.O. Box 150916
San Raphael, CA 94915
(800) 542-5227
http://www.dharmatrading.com
Silk dyes, silk fabrics

Fire Mountain Gems
1 Fire Mountain Way
Grants Pass, OR 97526-2373
(800) 423-2319
http://www.firemountaingems.com
Beads, beading supplies, Chinese coin replicas

Home Sew
P.O. Box 4099
Bethlehem, PA 18018-0099
(800) 344-4739
http://www.homesew.com
Cotton filler cord, Tassel-making kit, leather scraps, heirloom sewing supplies, trims, laces, threads

JCA, Inc.
35 Scales Ln.
Townsend, MA 01469
(978) 597-8794
Paternayan® Persian Wool threads

Kreinik Mfg. Co. Inc.
3106 Lord Baltimore Dr. Suite 101
Baltimore, MD 21244
(800) 537-2166
http://www.kreinik.com
Silk Serica® thread, iron-on and sew-on metallic braids and ribbons, Cord Twister and Corder Weight

Thai Silks
252 State St.
Los Altos, CA 94022
(800) 722-7455
http://www.thaisilks.com
Silk fabrics

Things Japanese
9805 N.E. 116th, Suite 7160
Kirkland, WA 98034-4248
http://www.silkthings.com
Silk dyes, Buttonhole Silk threads, spooled silks

Victoria Clayton
6448 Freeman Rd.
Byron, NY 14422-9720
(716) 548-2620
http://www.hand-dyedfibers.com
Hand-dyed Silk Perle & Spun Perle threads, Silk Chenille

YLI Corporation
161 W. Main St.
Rock Hill, SC 29730
(800) 296-8139
http://www.ylicorp.com
Silk ribbons, Quilting thread, Pearl Crown Rayon thread

Recommended Reading

"The Anatomy of a Doll," Susanna Oroyan, C&T Publishing, Inc., 1997.

"The Art of Manipulating Fabrics," Colette Wolff, Krause Publications, 1996.

"Chinese Knotting," Lydia Chen, Tuttle Publishing, 1982.

"The Complete Book of Floorcloths," Kathy Cooper and Jan Hersey, Lark Books, 1997.

"Tassels: The Fanciful Embellishment," Nancy Welch, Lark Books, 1992.

Other Books by this Author

"The Magic of Crazy Quilting, 2nd Edition"
This book covers the basics of crazy quilting, including 100 diagrammed embroidery stitches and 1,000 variations and combinations of them. It also includes embellishment how-to's for ribbonwork, silk ribbon embroidery, punchneedle, painting and dyeing and more. This is an essential reference for crazy quilting.

"Crazy Quilts by Machine"
This book includes methods for crazy quilting by machine, including patching, piecing, embroidery and embellishing. Also for the by-hand quilter, this book features designs for crazy quilts.

"Crazy Quilted Heirlooms & Gifts"
This book gives instructions for projects for the home and some great gift ideas. All are different ideas from those in "Crazy Quilt Décor."

"Motifs for Crazy Quilting"
This book includes hundreds of motifs, including ideas for designing your own. It shows how to transfer the motifs and shows many of them embroidered.